£1.75

A HOUSE OF MEMORIES

The author, Hana Raviv, at home in the drawing room of the Residence

A HOUSE OF MEMORIES

58 Avenue Road

HANA RAVIV

with a Foreword by

ISRAEL FINESTEIN

*To Tony & Martin
with my best wishes,
Hana Raviv,
4.3.98*

VALLENTINE MITCHELL
LONDON • PORTLAND, OR

First published in 1998 in Great Britain by
VALLENTINE MITCHELL
900 Eastern Avenue
London IG2 7HH

and in the United States of America by
VALLENTINE MITCHELL
c/o ISBS
5804 N.E. Hassalo Street
Portland, Oregon 97213-3644

British Library Cataloguing in Publication Data
A catalogue record for this book is available from the British Library

ISBN 0-85303-343-9 (cloth)
ISBN 0-85303-344-7 (paper)

Produced by A E Thompson Publishing Services London SW10 0AS
Typeset by MHL Typesetting Ltd Coventry
Printed in Great Britain by Bookcraft (Bath) Ltd, Midsomer Norton, Somerset

Contents

Acknowledgements

This book has been a voyage of discovery, a work of love, and I have received help and encouragement in completing it.

I am indebted first and foremost to Frank Cass who listened to my initial idea and encouraged me to put it to paper. I am also grateful to all who helped me in practical ways and have made invaluable suggestions, especially Stephen Massil and Rachel Joseph.

Special thanks go also to the Ambassadors and their families whom I have consulted freely and who have provided me with many of their recollections which sustain the narrative of this book.

The *Jewish Chronicle* archive and its staff have been constantly available for help and advice. Going through the old newspapers of many decades, it has been a fascinating journey for me and I am grateful to the JC staff for its help, and especially to Mrs Lynda Greenlick. I am particularly grateful to Sidney Harris for his photographs and advice on the illustrations and to those providing copies.

I am grateful also to the Trustees of the Eyre Estate who were able to provide me with details of the land register and the leases relating to the occupancy of 58 Avenue Road at different times.

My gratitude goes also to Gordon Hausman who shared in my excitement, to Professor Sir Martin Gilbert for his invaluable advice, and to Rachel Shavit-Bentwich who opened not only her home to me but also her life and personal recollections of the remarkable Bentwiches in Eretz Israel.

No. 58 Avenue Road today

Foreword

When an ambassador's wife decides to write a history of the ambassadorial Residence, two instant questions may fairly be asked. One is 'Why?'. The other is 'Why now?'. The plain fact is that Mrs Raviv has chosen her theme superbly well. And her timing is impeccable.

Since early in the eighteenth century the Eyre Estate has been the landlord of an extensive area in the Hampstead–St John's Wood region of London. The laying-out in the 1830s of a modernised and extended Finchley Road provided residents, businessmen, and visitors with a wide and more direct route between central London and the country to the north. In the 1840s the Eyre Estate built an avenue to connect that major road with Regent's Park. It was called Avenue Road, running from the northern gates of the royal park to what later became known as the Swiss Cottage junction. It was at that junction that the new Finchley Road began and where the horses would be changed. In 1868 the locality was crucially linked to the metropolitan railway system by the building of Swiss Cottage station.

Avenue Road was a broad green thoroughfare occupied by large houses set in their own grounds. It soon became a street of social fashion. Despite changes and some rebuilding, it has not lost its character. During the Second World War, the southern end suffered severe air-raid damage. That section, which did not include No. 58, was totally rebuilt. The rear of No. 58 sustained some serious damage and was repaired.

In the heyday of Theodor Herzl, No. 58 Avenue Road was the home of Herbert and Susannah (Susie) Bentwich and their talented family. In their welcoming and cultured household the founder of the political Zionist movement was a familiar and esteemed visitor. It was more than a social relationship. Bentwich was a solicitor and later a barrister and editor of the *Law Journal*. He was a man of courage and vision and energy, prominent in the intellectual and institutional life of the Jewish community of Britain. He was among the earliest devotees of political Zionism among the professional classes in the Jewish community. At a time when the movement met with 'fashionable' and influential opposition, he rallied to Herzl's call, introduced him to notable colleagues, and engaged in meetings with him and others to further his cause. For such encounters No. 58 Avenue Road was one of the natural centres.

It is remarkable that this house should one day have become the Residence of Israel's Ambassadors to the Court of St James. This would no doubt have been enough in itself to set alight the curiosity and imagination of Mrs Raviv in her capacity as hostess of that house. It represents a truly striking 'domestic' bridging of epochs. This book was written in the centenary year of the holding in Basle of the First Zionist Congress, a landmark in the history of the Jewish people, and is published as we prepare to meet the fiftieth anniversary of the Declaration of the State of Israel in 1948.

The St John's Wood Synagogue was established in 1876 in Abbey Road, in which street the Bentwiches lived before moving to Avenue Road. The building of the Hampstead Synagogue in 1892 indicated the continued northern growth of the metropolitan Jewish community. Bentwich was a leading figure in both congregations, a pioneer in the setting up of Hebrew and religion classes attached to the newer synagogues, as well as a consistent advocate of Jewish day school education. He was a founder and the first president of the Bnai Brith in Britain, a movement dedicated to the promotion of communal unity in action and which was to play a notable part in the progress of Anglo-Jewish Zionism.

In the nearby area of Maida Vale and Kilburn there had assembled in and around the 1890s a group of Jewish scholars and Jewishly learned professional men. Bentwich was a natural member of this significant milieu, which included Moses Gaster, Israel Zangwill and Solomon Schechter, all notable

Zionists in their own respective ways. As the group met from time to time in one another's homes, it is difficult to think that they did not meet at No. 58 Avenue Road. Bentwich's elder son, Norman, later Attorney-General in British Mandatory Palestine and Professor in International Relations at the Hebrew University of Jerusalem, was taught Jewish studies by Schechter, whose biography he was famously to write.

Herbert Bentwich had been an early recruit to the pre-Herzl body of *Hoveve Zion* (Lovers of Zion). There can be little doubt that the influence upon him of some members of the Maida Vale–Kilburn group, many of whom Herzl was to meet, was a factor in his new attachment to the more practical programme of political Zionism advanced by Herzl.

Hana Raviv's narrative is part of the history of Israel. At the same time it belongs to the story of Anglo-Jewry. A further strand of uniqueness in the many-sided tale of the house is that in no other land have Israel's succession of ambassadors occupied the self-same home throughout the whole of that half-century. The author recounts her recollections and the results of her enquiries and research, as wife and mother and as the ceaselessly supportive companion of a distinguished and popular Ambassador, an accomplished lady who in her own right has by universal acknowledgement contributed much to Israel and the Jewish community.

Her initial inspiration to embark upon this literary enterprise and her seeing it through to completion is furthermore not the least of her self-imposed roles in the strengthening of the cordial relations and mutual interests between her country and Britain. In all its changing and at times difficult patterns, that relationship has had throughout, as part of its hub, the address which is the subject of this work.

Thus it is that these pages bring together a family history and a revolution in Jewish life and thought. No. 58 is both a home and a Residence. Its outer design and inner structure discharge effectively the task connoted by the latter capacity. It certainly has the quality of an ambassadorial residence. Yet its spaciousness somehow manages to evince none of the pretentions sometimes associated with such a feature. It has an easy elegance. It is reflected in Mrs Raviv's distinctively personal style, as she assembles all the echoes in her telling chronicle. It is sometimes sad, sometimes joyous, always authentic.

Here are mirrored the visits of politicians from Israel, Westminster and elsewhere, the Independence Day celebrations, the communal events, the sombre commemorations, the delightful garden parties, the private and public occasions of immense variety, in the 50 year 'diary' of a house of renown.

For my wife and myself, the event which in a wholly special way catches the nature of that renown and the texture of its notability was the visit of the Russian Ambassador in the early aftermath of the uncongealing of the old Soviet doors. This genial diplomat joined in the musical evening at which the centre-piece was the playing by a Russian Jewish family ensemble. It all represented a massive transformation of far-reaching consequence to the State of Israel.

We remembered Herzl's 'If you will it, it is no dream'. The Herbert Bentwiches would have rejoiced. Their home under Mrs Bentwich was much given to music. The imprint of that vivid Jewish image near the close of this century of heartbreak and renewal is indelible. And we remembered Herzl again – 'certainly in 50 years ...'. Here is the story of a house of Jewish memories and promise, from the pen of one of the gracious moulders of its living fame.

Israel Finestein
17 Tevet 5758
15 January 1998

I T WAS A LOVELY October day in 1993, in the early hours of a warm evening, when we entered 58 Avenue Road which would be our home for the next few years. From the airport we had been driven directly to the Embassy, where many friends and leaders of the community had been waiting to welcome us. But then to the Residence.

It was not the first time we had gone through the door of this magnificent house, but our feelings and our thoughts on this occasion were different – a house steeped in all our history because it had been the Ambassador's residence almost since the beginning! If only these walls could speak, could tell us what they have witnessed, seen and heard. I could not let go of this thought – if it could be told . . ., if . . . all the joys, the tears, the interesting people who have gathered here, the music, the functions, the worries and the pains during tense times in Israel, or those happy days of joy and relief that followed the Six Day War, or the tragic days after the shooting of Shlomo Argov, or the first historic visit of the Jordanian Ambassador after the breakthrough of the Oslo Agreements and the conclusion of peace with Jordan – the thought of what this house could tell haunted me. I became absorbed in detective work investigating the past of the house.

Then, just by chance, reading a biography of Herbert Bentwich, I discovered to my great astonishment that 58 Avenue Road has not only had a fascinating role throughout the history of the State of Israel, it played an even more fascinating role in the past.

Jewish life in this house was intertwined from the beginning with the history of the Zionist movement in Britain and with the life of one of Anglo-Jewry's most prominent families – the Bentwich family. So this house, with the Embassy at 2 Palace Green, Kensington, has shared centre stage not only in representing Israel in Great Britain but also in the life of the Jewish community of a hundred years ago at the emergence of

1

the Zionist movement in England. This was the inspiration for my starting research which has caused me to trace the London life of the Bentwich family and also their homes in Eretz Israel where the impact of the force of Zionism on their personal and their public lives can be vividly appreciated.

Time and again, I am asked by many visitors to the house, what is its history? What is the background? Were all the previous Israeli ambassadors in residence here?

It is one of the more familiar houses in the community, but one of the least known. I found it fascinating when I told a group of people gathered in the beautiful and gracious drawing room for a function of the Friends of the Hebrew University that probably in the same room were held the first meetings during which the idea of creating a Jewish university in Palestine took root. What a historic coincidence to be gathered in this room where the Hebrew University was conceived, thriving and so renowned as it is to-day with its four campuses at Mount Scopus (the original site), Givat Ram, Hadassah – the Medical school – and Rehovot – the Agricultural school – and 22,000 students, and to remember that here embryonic ideas for its establishment were nurtured.

At many of the functions held in the Residence there is music, performed mainly by Israeli musicians. Well, these walls heard a lot of music during the Bentwich period. How can we not remember that Thelma Yellin, née Bentwich, was born in this house. The whole family filled the house with music, but particularly Thelma who was a gifted cellist, a player of chamber music with a scholarship to the Royal College of Music, a most beloved student of Pablo Casals; later in her life in Palestine she was a pioneer of chamber music – and it all began on Sunday gatherings in this very house.

From my first days after arriving at Avenue Road, I decided to open the house and let all groups who work and support Israel enjoy its spacious rooms, its atmosphere. In this book, I would like to open the door of the house also to the many who would like to tour it, not only in the present but also through its glorious past days. I hope and I wish it to be my modest way of thanking the warm and noble Jewish community in Britain, on the eve of the fiftieth anniversary of Israel's independence, for making us, all representatives of the

The drawing room of the Residence

State of Israel, feel part of a big family, participating in the wonderful journey of the realisation of the Zionist dream.

F OR ISRAELIS LONDON is probably the most sought after place for a posting of a few years. It has many virtues and great appeal but also some slight 'disadvantages' for the Ambassador, like being geographically 'on the way' to somewhere. So why not stop off on the way to Paris or to New York and enjoy a few days in London. Israelis adore London, feel at ease with the language, the theatre, the way of life. After all, we were once part of the British Empire. So one is visited by journalists, Members of Knesset and other public servants, and of course by friends, friends of friends, family, or neighbours, 'en route' to or from somewhere. Many a time, the Ambassador has to say farewell to or meet a government Minister in transit at the airport, or go to the theatre with the wife of another Minister. He has to be ready to entertain, help, organise schedules and meetings, or sometimes, at short notice, hold a dinner in someone's honour.

The Residence is always ready to welcome guests. Although the public areas are pleasant and functional, the private quarters are surprisingly limited – which is a blessing in disguise since it means that official guests have to be booked into a hotel. It is very complicated to have as overnight guests a Minister and his aides, and all the security people. It is much more practical for the Embassy to take a whole floor at a hotel, where an office and all the security provisions, unfortunately so much part of our life today, can be organised smoothly.

The house can, however, accommodate large parties, dinners and luncheons, concerts or lectures for 80 or 90 guests, and garden parties, when the lawn can be covered by a marquee and hold more than 800 people, as is done at the annual Independence Day reception.

As I have said, after our arrival in London, we decided to open the Residence for the use of all the Anglo-Jewish organisations connected with Israel. After all, it is a 'little Israeli territory in the midst of the UK'.

My diary was soon filled with bookings for a wide range of functions: concerts, dinners and garden parties; demonstrations of Middle Eastern cookery by Claudia Roden; concerts by the famous Israeli duo Bracha Eden and Alexander Tamir, or the Schidlof Quartet; recitals by accomplished young pianists; a whole choir of Russian immigrants (the Gefen

The Gefen Choir of Russian olim *from Tel Aviv, 1994*

4

Choir); evenings of light drama and performances by the Israeli actress Dalia Friedland and her friend, the English actress Anna Croft; even a football game on the lawn with Ronnie Rosenthal and a class of youngsters from a school in Holon who had won a trip to England and so visited the Residence in their turn.

The list is long and the diversity of functions exciting. Once, for ten days we were hosts to Israel's only set of quintuplets, all boys celebrating their bar-mitzvah with the London community. Once again, there was a football game in the garden with Ronnie Rosenthal, followed by a Friday Night meal with all the families that helped in the celebration of the five-fold bar-mitzvah, headed by the David Khalili family. I should like to dwell on some of the most significant occasions that have taken place in the Residence in our time.

A tribute to a friend of Israel

I met Maria Ines Curej de Costa Barbosa, wife of the Brazilian Ambassador, and found that she was the granddaughter of Oswaldo Aranha. In 1947 he was foreign minister of Brazil and Ambassador to the General Assembly of the United Nations, where he was President of the crucial sessions debating the Partition Plan. On 29 November 1947, the Plan which declared in favour of the establishment of a Jewish state and an Arab state in Palestine was finally adopted. Abba Eban describes Aranha's decisive role in the adoption of this Resolution:

5

A reception for the wife of the Brazilian Ambassador, 1994

The President of the General Assembly, Brazil's Oswaldo Aranha, was a man of passionate and romantic disposition, who was religiously exalted by the idea of Jewish statehood ... When the speech-makers and their audiences were exhausted, he revived our hopes.

Ambassador Aranha found a way to postpone the meeting for two days. Meanwhile, we could carry on the work behind the scenes, to persuade more countries to vote in favour of the Resolution – and the rest is history. On the 29th November 1947, the dramatic moment arrived. After the vote, President Aranha rapped his gavel, and announced – thirty three in favour, thirteen against, ten abstentions.

There is no doubting how instrumental Aranha had been in the saga of the establishment of the State of Israel. A cultural centre has been established in his memory in Israel, and Kibbutz Bror-Chail, founded by young people from Brazil. Here in London I decided to pay homage to the memory of Oswaldo Aranha by inviting many women, representatives of the Jewish community, to an afternoon tea in honour of

Madame Curej de Costa Barbosa. Ruth Rosen, the actress and a good friend, read from Abba Eban's book *Personal Witness*, and I introduced the granddaughter of a wonderful friend of the Jewish people. It was a moving afternoon for everybody.

Abba Eban's birthday

Another outstanding event at the house was the celebration of the eightieth birthday of one of Israel's most revered statesmen and diplomats, Abba Eban.

Eban began his career and close involvement with Zionism in London. We felt it was therefore most appropriate to celebrate his eightieth birthday here. A long list of guests joined us for dinner, among them Lord Mishcon, a childhood friend of Eban, the Minister of State for Foreign Affairs, the Rt Hon. Douglas Hogg, the Lord Chief Justice, Lord Taylor, Sir Martin and Lady Gilbert, Alan Yentob, Sir Claus and Lady Moser, the Hon. Greville Janner and Mrs Janner, and many others. The excitement was great because seated at the top

Guests at Abba Eban's eightieth birthday party (left to right) the Rt Hon. Douglas Hogg, H.E. Ambassador Fouad Ayoub, H.E. Ambassador Moshe Raviv, with Abba Eban (in front)

Guests at Abba Eban's eightieth birthday party (left to right) H.E. Ambassador Raviv, Lord Chief Justice Lord Taylor, Lord Mishcon – a childhood friend of Eban and his wife

table next to the guest of honour was the Ambassador of Jordan, by now a good friend, H.E. Ambassador Fouad Ayoub and his charming wife Maria. The atmosphere was indeed festive, and Eban replied to all the other speakers in a sparkling and, as always, brilliant way. No-one would believe for a moment that in front of us were two octogenerians, Lord Mishcon and Abba Eban, both marvellous speakers with

Guests at Abba Eban's eightieth birthday party (left to right) Sir Martin Gilbert and Lady Gilbert, Mrs Susie Eban and Hana Raviv

such spectacular lives of experience behind them. The recital before dinner was given by a gifted young Israeli pianist, Shlomi Shaban. The late Lord Taylor, himself an accomplished pianist, remarked how much he enjoyed the performance.

I must confess that we break with British protocol after dinner. On many of the occasions when we are invited to private homes, men and women still separate after the meal, the men to stay with their port and cigars and round-table discussion and the women to follow the hostess 'to powder one's nose' and indulge in 'women's talk'. Well, it is a strange habit for us Israelis, coming from a country especially proud of equality between the sexes and informality in general. So we have given up the practice without, I hope, offending any of our guests.

Leader of the Opposition

During their tour of duty diplomats try not to get involved in the local political scene and its struggles but have, as a constant objective, the building of good relations and understanding with both the Government and the Opposition. Thus we always maintained good relations with prominent members of the Labour Party. They visited Israel on several occasions. During one Christmas recess, the late John Smith, when leader of the Opposition, took his wife and three grown-up daughters on a combined business and leisure trip to Israel. Following the official meetings in Jerusalem and Tel Aviv, they all went down to the Dead Sea to relax for a few days. On their return to London, we held a dinner for about thirty people to hear his impressions and thoughts after his first visit to our country. Among the guests were members of the Shadow Cabinet together with some prominent Jewish communal leaders. There was talk of the good relations between the Labour Party in Israel and the Labour Party in Britain. John Smith described his 'deep and gratifying impressions' of the economic prosperity in Israel, and the optimistic atmosphere there. He was 'very impressed and moved' by the deep commitment of the Government and of the people of Israel, to the Peace Process, and the prospects of development in the whole area as a dividend of the peace. In his letter of thanks after the dinner, he said:

> I write to thank you very much for having Elisabeth and myself to your home as guests of honour at last night's dinner. We enjoyed being amongst friends. Thank you for helping make my visit to Israel such a success. I am confident that we can build ever closer links between our countries.

I record these three events that took place in our Residence, in order to allow a glimpse into the life of this house which has shown the flag of Israel for the past fifty years.

WE HAD BEEN HERE many times over the years but I never had any premonition that we would one day have the privilege of knowing the house so intimately. Then, from the first days of our settling in, I felt the need to write about the Ambassadors who had lived here, to give an impression of their lives here, to note the impact of events that reveal their character and style in the conduct of public affairs, the joyful days and the tragic experiences, the music, the conversations that these walls have heard.

However, when having tea one day with our friends Judge Finestein and his wife Marion, a book was shown to me: *Herbert Bentwich – the Pilgrim Father*, and in it the picture of the whole Bentwich family on the front steps of 58 Avenue Road in 1910. To my great amazement and excitement, I learnt that 58 Avenue Road cradles not only the whole history of modern Israel through the experience of its ambassadors in residence here but also the spectacular history of the Zionist Movement in this country going back to the days of Herzl and his connections with the Bentwich family a century ago.

The Bentwich family in London

In 1881 Herbert Bentwich married Susanna Solomon (1862–1915) and they set up home first of all in Abbey Road to the west of St John's Wood. Jewish families had been moving into

10

the area for some time. Their first seven children were born there. By 1892 they needed a more spacious house, to allow room for the growing family, and found one on the east side of St John's Wood at 58 Avenue Road with a lease of 50 years, time enough to see them all through. The move, though not of great distance, was venturesome in that most of their acquaintance in the area lived along the route of the Edgware Road – Maida Vale and Kilburn High Road. In Avenue Road, with its proximity to Swiss Cottage and the Finchley Road, they were taking up, for a Jewish family, new territory. The house at No. 58, known then as The Holm (all Herbert Bentwich's letters carry the name at the head), appears on maps from 1864. By 1892, when developments to the west of

The Holm – the original house at No. 58 Avenue Road

11

the area were under way, Avenue Road was still quiet and semi-rural. The street was lined with trees, and along it were only a few large country houses, their gardens backing onto open space.

St John's Wood at the turn of the century

The very names of the streets are full of delight: Oak Tree Road, Elm Tree Road, Grove End Road, St John's Wood Park, Abbey Gardens, Acacia Road ... Artists, writers, painters used to live here. The area between Avenue Road and Hampstead Village was a vast field on the maps until the 1880s. Sheep and cattle used to graze where today is the busy Swiss Cottage intersection. Sir Edwin Landseer, famous later as a painter of animals, used to walk to Hampstead and on the way, admiring the cows, would sketch the grazing animals. In his book of 1913, *St John's Wood, its Houses, its Haunts and its Celebrities*, Alan Eyre writes:

> What other London district has had so many artists, and literary associations, since the days of the Prince Regent? Huxley, Thomas Hood, George Eliot, Herbert Spencer, Douglas Gerrold, Romney, Tissot, actors, musicians, and others.

The Eyre family still owns much of the St John's Wood and Finchley area. Stella Margetson's more recent account, *St John's Wood: an Abode of Love and the Arts*, records the growth of the area and the myriad names of artists, writers and celebrities who have lived there, but she does not cite diplomats and politicians, and I would add to her account of musicians the name of August Wilhelmj who also lived in Avenue Road and taught the Bentwich children the violin.

The writing of Jewish settlement in the area would make an agreeable addition to these accounts. Norman Bentwich, in his Presidential lecture to the Jewish Historical Society in 1960, records the 'wandering' scholars of his youth, referring to the coterie of scholars and journalists who led the intellectual invigoration of Anglo-Jewry from the mid-1880s into the new century and lived in the 'half-Bohemian area of Kilburn and St John's Wood', and provides useful topographical

12

details along the way: Joseph Jacobs, Leopold Greenberg and Solomon Schechter away near West Hampstead, Asher Myers (editor of the *Jewish Chronicle*) at the top end of Abbey Road, Arthur Davis, Israel Zangwill and Solomon J. Solomon straddling Kilburn High Road, Isidore Harris at Maida Vale, Israel Abrahams near Little Venice.

Jewish families had begun living in the area beyond Marylebone (between Little Venice, Kilburn, Hampstead and Regent's Park) from the 1860s. The Central Synagogue (originally a branch of the Great Synagogue at Aldgate) opened in Great Portland Street in 1855 and Bayswater Synagogue opened in 1863. The United Synagogue consecrated a new cemetery at Willesden in 1873. The St John's Wood Synagogue on Abbey Road, where Herbert Bentwich was first a member, was consecrated in 1882, having been founded in 1876, and by 1904 had 378 seatholders. Hampstead Synagogue, of which Herbert was a founder member in 1892 when he worked with Harris Lebus (the furniture tycoon who lived in Netherhall Gardens) on the plans for the building, had 464 seatholders. The Spanish & Portuguese Jews' Congregation moved from their 'West End' branch at Bryanstone Street to Lauderdale Road, Maida Vale, in 1895. Margery Bentwich records the younger children going for religious instruction to Dayan Lazarus's class at neighbouring Brondesbury Synagogue, established in 1905.

The first tavern, at what we now call Swiss Cottage, was built in 1840, the Swiss style being much in fashion due to the popularity of a new opera *Le Chalet* by Adolf Adam. By 1856 it had become a terminus for horse-drawn buses, with a 'direct express line' to the Bank and City, and changing of the horses took place just at the top end of Avenue Road. By 1900, when the Bentwiches were firmly established in Avenue Road, the flat fare was 6d, and we can presume that Mr Bentwich, Barrister-at-Law, Member of the Inner Temple, used this express service quite often on his way to chambers in the City, as did Norman Bentwich to St Paul's School. The girls went to nearby South Hampstead High School.

From No. 58 one could see directly to Primrose Hill, but tranquillity could hardly have prevailed, for the ongoing march of urbanisation soon saw the opening of Elsworthy

Road and its homes set out in garden-suburb style (retained to this day) early in the new century. Here was their 'Garden of Eden', fruit trees bordering the lawn, elderberry and almond trees, lilac bushes, chestnuts, a swing hung between the trees for the children. In the basement, there was a large sunny kitchen, and a large playroom, a weekday dining room for the large family of children and their friends. On the first floor was the mother's bedroom and the schoolroom, which served as a classroom for the younger children until their teens. A gate at the top of the flight of stairs (still in place today) was to prevent the babies from escaping downstairs.

The Bentwich family at home

The house was great for entertainment, bar-mitzvahs, family and communal gatherings, meetings of the 'Wanderers', when Herbert took a turn as host for the evening, Schechter would hold forth and Joseph Jacobs would bring fairy stories along for the children – and later the daughters' debuts and concerts. The atmosphere in the house was dominated by two factors: the arts and Zionism. St John's Wood claims an English association and impetus for early Zionism with the publication of George Eliot's *Daniel Deronda* in 1875.

The arts – the sounds of music always filled the house, the beauty and elegance of decorations, from stained-glass windows to the frieze of casts of the Elgin Marbles, oil paintings, sketches by the Victorian masters, Phoenician glass brought back from the pilgrimage of 1897, and photographs of Palestine. Many English and Hebrew sayings, like 'sow not, reap nought' or 'the day is short and the work is great', even snakes in bottles and reptiles from the Dead Sea area could be found around the house. But the art that reigned above all was music. Every one of the children took up an instrument, and practised each day, starting before school at 6.30 in the morning!

Mrs Bentwich was a pianist of high standard, and she instilled in her children the love of music. Achievement was a strong factor. The eleven children naturally divided into bands

of three, one of them playing the piano, the second the violin and the third the cello. On Shabbat, they all welcomed and accepted a silence of the instruments. As Norman Bentwich recalls years later: 'On Shabbat the music was silenced, and it was observed, prepared and conducted in a most joyous way, with shining silver, flowers, each child in the best clothing, father in his brown velvet coat, like a king in his kingdom.' Around the table there were always guests, amazed at the ritual and the Jewish custom, the loveliness of the children and the dignity of the Shabbat dinner.

The Bentwich Family in 1913 on the steps of 58 Avenue Road (Courtesy: Mrs Viola Hacohen)

15

Our home was the meeting place for a varied group of Christian sympathisers with the Zionist cause: Holman Hunt, the Pre-Raphaelite painter, who painted in Jerusalem, Colonel Condor, the Archaeological Director of the Palestine Exploration Fund, and others.

Our home attracted also a cosmopolitan group of Jewish Zionists, ardent, argumentative, from all parts of the world. They would come on Shabbat, and were startled by my father's beautiful singing of the long Hebrew Grace after the meal.

Herbert Bentwich and his wife Susanna had eleven children in all; four of them were born during the years they lived in Avenue Road. In 1893, Hebe was born, in 1895 Thelma, in 1899 Carmel – and finally in 1902, the second son, Joseph. The older son, Norman, had been born in 1883 when they were still living in Abbey Road. One can understand from the names of the last four children the ideals of the family at this period. Hebe and Thelma were born after trips to Venice and Norway, Carmel and Joseph reflected growing love and involvement in the Zionist movement. By the year 1897, Herbert Bentwich could look with pride not only at the 'Procession', that famous celebration of Queen Victoria's diamond jubilee, where he had 'ten seats secured' to watch the festivities, but also on his lovely and glorious family.

The Zionist vision

Herbert and Susanna Bentwich were at the heart of the early history of the Zionist movement in Britain. Herbert was born in 1856 in Whitechapel, his father from a recent immigrant family, his mother from one of the older Anglo-Jewish families settled in Bedford since the eighteenth century, famous as the home of John Bunyan, author of *Pilgrim's Progress*, a book imbibed by English schoolchildren for generations. Bentwich was educated in both the Jewish tradition and the English, such as was sought after by advanced-thinking Anglo-Jewish families of the time. At University College London he won the Hollier Hebrew Scholarship and gained prizes in jurisprudence and in English law. His choice of studies was from the beginning meant 'to be devoted to communal activity, and he embarked on his profession and his communal work with equal gusto', as recalled by his son Norman.

One has to remember that the protracted struggle for Jewish emancipation was perceived to have achieved its goal when Lionel de Rothschild secured admission to the House of Commons in 1858 followed by several other Jewish members; the abiding character of Jewish public life was a sense of double duty – loyally to serve Jewry and the country which had accorded Jews equal opportunity. Herbert Bentwich was one of those convinced that he had to dedicate his life to the service of his people, and to the public life of Britain.

One of the heroes of his life was Sir Moses Montefiore whom he was privileged to meet in person on many occasions. The spirit of the legendary Montefiore, an English Jew proudly speaking up for his people on the international stage, was the inspiration of his life. Then there was Emile Zola, whose intervention in the Dreyfus Affair in France was dramatic. 'The Dreyfus case played an important part in our family life, from 1897, as it did in the life of Herzl', wrote Norman. 'It was hotly discussed in our home. Zola was a hero to my father, after he published the famous article "J'accuse". His portrait, and that of Captain Dreyfus, hang in the library.' Here Norman continues with his memories that thrilled me, as a reader today, and as a resident of 58 Avenue Road:

> Herzl was an occasional visitor in our home, and his magnificent presence, royal dignity and beautiful voice, made him a hero for us children. He brought something new and exciting to Judaism.

Herzl, the legendary, majestic figure, came through the doors of this house. He walked on this site, maybe sat in the garden trying to gain souls for his new plan for a Jewish home in Palestine – and here we are today, representing the state that he dreamt of, and struggled so much to convince everyone of: 'If you will it, it is no dream'.

Herzl, who encountered opposition in many European countries, visited England frequently, and found in Herbert

Bentwich and his group of Maccabaeans (established in 1891) enthusiastic support. This group included notable Jews of the period: Solomon Schechter, Solomon J. Solomon, Israel Zangwill, Joseph Jacobs, Albert Goldsmid and Lucien Wolf. In 1897, Herbert organised a group of 20 who travelled for a visit of two weeks in Palestine, glorified by the title 'The Maccabaean Pilgrimage'. They were fired by their first encounter with the ancient country. The group set out on 6 April 1897 with a sense of ecstasy – all wearing a medallion, with the motifs of the Menorah and the Star of David combined. Zangwill joined the party but Schechter was unable to do so because of a more momentous mission to Cairo during that winter to secure the Genizah manuscripts for Cambridge University Library.

In a letter to Bentwich, Herzl gave his blessing to the 'Pilgrimage' though he himself had yet to visit Palestine. (He did so a few years later when he had a dramatic encounter with the German Kaiser at the Jaffa Gate into Jerusalem!)

The trip is described in detail in the annals of those days. By boat, by carriage, by railway and by camel, on the eve of Passover, April 1897, they arrived at Jaffa. The French railway from Jaffa to Jerusalem had just opened. They also visited Mikveh Israel, the Dead Sea, the Judaean Mountains and Tiberias. The impression left by the Pilgrimage both in Palestine and in Britain was tremendous. To the Jews of Palestine it revived memories of Montefiore's visits in former generations. The Jewish newspapers counted it as one of the 'outstanding events of the era that brought a widespread interest in the Zionist Congress in Basle'. This trip also fired the imagination of the young Bentwiches and gave them the idea of making their future lives in Palestine.

Herbert returned as a hero to his family. Pictures of Palestine lined the staircase, joining photographs of earlier trips to Italy. Though pressed by Herzl, he did not go as a delegate to the first Basle Congress (in August) but he went to the second and two years later took Norman with him to the third. From this time on, the house was filled with enthusiasm for Zionism, and was frequented by Zionists from central and eastern Europe. He did not at this stage consider a move of his own family to Palestine, and only contemplated this in later years when his children went to build their lives there. Symbolically, their country house in Birchington, Kent, during that period was called Carmelcourt and was his English Zion, an overture to the future. In the garden at Carmelcourt, on the Kent coast, he flew both the Union Jack and Zionist flags. In the dining room the motto on the wall was 'If not now, when?' 'How splendid, a Jewish Colony on English soil!' exclaimed Herzl's son Hans when visiting the place. It was in preparation for their Carmel Court at Zichron Ya'akov in Palestine.

In 1898, Herbert Bentwich was the organiser of a committee for a joint conference of the English 'Lovers of Zion' (*Hoveve Zion*) and the political Zionists. It was a turning point in the practical development of the 'Jewish national idea' in Britain, which at once inspired great enthusiasm among the masses for the Herzlian plan of a national home in Zion. He addressed the conference, representing Herzl, and spoke of the promotion and establishment of more colonies in Palestine. Herbert was a member of the Political Advisory Committee (which included Harry Sacher and Ahad Ha'am under the leadership of Weizmann and Sokolov). As a lawyer, he advised Herzl in the formulation of many of the early Zionist documents, such as the charter of the First Jewish Colonial Trust (a forerunner of the Bank Leumi), still to be seen at the Zionist Archives in Jerusalem. During the First World War, he drafted a scheme for the future of Palestine after the War which was adopted by the Zionist Committee. It included equality of civic rights for all the inhabitants of the country, equality of national and religious groups, recognition of the Jewish population as a community with distinct national and religious character, proposals for proportionate representation of both the Jewish and non-Jewish population in local government, recognition of Hebrew as an official language, autonomy of the Jewish people in religious matters, removal of restrictions on immigration, naturalisation of Jewish settlers, and the recognition of their right to purchase land for colonisation.

Here we have a foretaste of the Mandate. He was always ahead of his time. As he was among the first in Anglo-Jewry to support Herzl, so he was farseeing in his anticipation of the complexities of life in post-Ottoman Palestine and he put forward moderate proposals for the resolution of the problems ahead. He was part of the group whose discussions on the question of a Jewish homeland in Palestine with the British Government led to the Balfour Declaration of November 1917, and he joined with them in saying the blessing of '*Shehechianu*' on that momentous occasion.

Herbert Bentwich lived part of his Zionist dreams through his children who, in 1913, went to settle in Eretz Israel. His daughters Nita and Muriel built their homes in Zichron Ya'akov, while his son Norman, who became Attorney General during the Mandate, lived in Jerusalem.

In 1913 the remaining Bentwiches moved from 58 Avenue Road to the home vacated by Nita in Cavendish Road, overlooking Lord's Cricket Ground. In a letter to his parents, Norman wrote:

> We have all moved forward a little during the year, carrying out the idea you have handed down to us. And though physically we are more scattered than we have been before, I feel that we are as close knit, and closer-knit than ever. The family love not only holds us fast together, but it gives a certain unity to all our work and our strivings.

Thus in 1913, the chapter of the life of the Bentwich family in Avenue Road came to an end.

Among all the Zionist causes that Herbert Bentwich took an interest in from those years, the most compelling was the idea of establishing a 'Jewish university' in Jerusalem. By 1913, this idea was firmly rooted among British Jews as a basis for the cultural development of Palestine. One of the meetings held in this house brought Sir Philip Magnus, MP, to join with Herbert in advocating the need for 'a university that should provide refuge for Jewish intellectuals excluded from institutions of learning in Europe'. He lived to see the foundation of the Hebrew University in Jerusalem in 1925, and he also established a fund for student dormitories on Mount Scopus.

Herbert Bentwich finally went to settle in Palestine in the spring of 1929, a few years after the death of his beloved wife

Susie. His last three years were that stormy period of Arab attacks and the conflict with British officials over restrictions on Jewish immigration. Nevertheless, he entered with zest into political life and never lost sight of his goal and ideal of a homeland. He was known as 'Old Bentwich' to distinguish him from his son, 'Young Bentwich' who, by 1931, had accepted a Professorship of International Law at the Hebrew University. Until his death in 1932, 'Old Bentwich' remained hurt and humiliated by the turn of events in the relations between Britain and the Jews of Palestine and the restrictions on immigration. He was a believer in the strong bonds between Britain and the Jews.

Thelma Yellin

Going back to the period of Avenue Road, I would like to recall another member of the Bentwich family, who contributed so much to the enrichment of the life of the Yishuv. This is Thelma Bentwich, better known to Israelis as Thelma Yellin. Everyone in Israel knows the Thelma Yellin Music School. She was born in this house in 1895. Born and raised on the borderline of the nineteenth and twentieth centuries, between Victorian highmindedness and modern broadmindedness, between the strict Jewish traditionalism of her father and the English liberal romanticism of her mother, she bore great social and personal pressures. In her late teens, she suffered a breakdown and was sent to Palestine to join her sisters and brother to recuperate there.

Like all the Bentwich children, she took to the cello naturally, with talent and determination. Their home was a salon, visited by famous musicians. Misha Elman made it his second home. Thelma used to play quartets and continued her studies at the Royal College of Music in 1911. Pablo Casals became the dominating influence in her life as a musician and she studied under his instruction.

When she joined her two sisters, Nita and Muriel, and her brother Norman, reaching Jerusalem in May 1920, she immediately became part of the young musical scene there. She was a pioneer of chamber music. She gave her first concert in Tel Aviv, then still but a suburb of Jaffa, in 1920 playing

Thelma Bentwich playing the cello, 1908, from a painting by Muriel Bentwich (Courtesy: Mrs Viola Hacohen)

Bruch's 'Kol Nidrei' and a Corelli sonata. There she met young Eliezer Yellin, the son of David Yellin who, together with Eliezer Ben-Yehuda had dedicated his life to the revival of the Hebrew language. Eliezer proposed marriage to her on the night after the concert.

With Eliezer's encouragement, Thelma decided to continue her life in music after their marriage and that was to be until her last day – a life of commitment to music through concerts, teaching and radio broadcasts to youngsters. Their house in Rehavia was always open to musicians. She combined motherhood and musical life with ease. She organised the famous Jerusalem String Quartet, giving weekly chamber concerts. She played a pioneering role in the development of music and musical education in Israel for nearly 40 years. Professor Partosh, director of the Israel Academy of Music, said by way of tribute to her: 'She did not live to see the school that has been her cherished dream, but we have given this school her name. The young Israeli musician should try to live up to her expectations, and honour her name.'

And Thelma Yellin-Bentwich was born in what is now the Residence!

Zichron Ya'akov: The Bentwich estate 'Beit Lange'

Through the thick pine trees, olives, the lush foliage of the eucalyptus, the cypresses and palms lining the road, I saw for the first time the Lange House in Zichron Ya'akov as it was intended, 'an English garden in the promised Land'.

Rachel Shavit, née Bentwich, daughter of Joseph Bentwich, at Beit Lange, 1997

I spent the whole of a hot July Shabbat as the guest of Rachel Shavit-Bentwich who inherited the house and studio of her aunt the painter Muriel Bentwich who died in 1981. Rachel is the daughter of Joseph Bentwich, the last-born and younger son of Herbert and Susanna Bentwich, born in No. 58 in 1902. Rachel Shavit told me how the Bentwiches had wanted a twelfth child to make up their tribesworth – a romantic notion! – and that Susanna was expecting twins but lost them and in fact died of the complications in 1915, although this is not spelt out in the family biographies.

She explained that the name Bentwich derives from Herbert's family name of Ben-Dov, the Bendowitches. Herbert grew up a second-generation Whitechapel Jew and was very careful with words and their meaning (in lawyerly fashion), thus he preferred to be known as Ben-Tov-Ish; the English version Bentwich has a Hebrew meaning (son of a good man).

Rachel Shavit is a serious painter in her own right (carrying the Solomon gcnes). She is also a lecturer on art and the long-serving chairperson of the Tel Aviv Painters and Sculptors Association.

She was my hostess for the day and ready to share with me all her personal memories and knowledge of the Bentwich family. She only warned me that her stories would reflect all aspects of this saga, not just the beautiful side of the story but

23

also the unpleasant turns that beset the family over the years. And what a family saga it is. It awaits real research and a sense of the life of these remarkable generations intertwined with the annals of the last hundred years of Zionism and the Jewish renaissance.

Her father, Joseph, who became during the Mandate Director of the Department of Education and later Inspector-General, never wrote a biography, but he was the author of many of the textbooks Israeli schoolchildren used to learn English at school. In the last months of his life, the family was able to ask him about and learn many stories of the past.

He recalled how he celebrated his bar-mitzvah at a big party at their London home (by then Cavendish Road); how he walked escorted by his parents and in a top-hat to the Portuguese Synagogue in Lauderdale Road. His mother, from an affluent artistic family, gave up prospects of a musical career when she married. She and Herbert reached an agreement on their children's upbringing: she would direct all her energy and talents to their musical and artistic education, he would instil Judaism, tradition and the love of Zion. The truth is that Susanna could never understand or share in the Zionist fervour of her husband and children. She never visited Palestine, she never saw the fascination of the Zionist dream (as was also the case with the wives of many of the Zionist leaders, particularly Herzl's wife). This created much tension and was the occasion of repeated frustration in the family but this was well covered by the great love and strength of character of the Bentwiches! They achieved a divine state of balance that bridged their differences.

Rachel told me again the stories of the children being born in groups of three, so as to be able to play music in trios! Practising every morning before school, they sang together as a choir in a perfect musical manner, especially on Shabbat and Holy Days. They used to sing and speak in the correct Sephardi manner, even in those early days of the revival of Hebrew speech! The *ex libris* in Herbert's books at Avenue Road had the Hebrew inscription of the 'stag rampant' and other symbols of Judaism, such as the word 'Zion' on the rising sun on the horizon (Herbert's Hebrew name was Zvi Hirsh, a deer).

24

Solomon J. Solomon, Susanna's brother, had a great influence on the Bentwich children who painted, especially Muriel. He was a fashionable portrait-painter and became an RA in 1896. In a work, *Conversation Piece*, which normally hangs in Leighton House, Kensington, he depicts the Solomon family salon with Susanna at the piano, a work that highlights the family's rich social standing. He was also, incidentally, a pioneer of naval camouflage in the First World War; many British warships were spared from attack as a result of his ingenuity. But it was also he who invited Herzl to be the guest speaker at the 'Maccabaeans Club' where Herbert became deeply involved with and devoted to Herzl.

On his first and famous pilgrimage to Palestine in 1897, Herbert Bentwich included both a *shohet* (a ritual butcher) and a *hazan* (a cantor) in the group. He remained a practising Jew all his life. This was Herbert's concept of Zionism: pilgrimage. He saw the revival of the Jewish national home, not as a political state like all other states, but as a spiritual revival. He believed in a Pilgrim's Zionism (Asher Ginsberg, Ahad Ha'am, the prophet of spiritual Zionism who lived in nearby Hampstead, was one of his friends and a frequent visitor to his home). Herbert had all his later life a walking stick marked with silver rings, one for each of his pilgrimages to Eretz Israel. This stick is now in the possession of his great grandson Ari, Rachel's son. This also explains why his children, when writing about the life of their father, entitled their biography *The Pilgrim Father*.

Rachel returns to the story of her father Joseph. Born as number 11 and the youngest with nine sisters and an older brother, he was brought up more by his sisters. They used to spoil him, teach him, dress him in a kilt (which he hated). When he was nearing the end of his studies at Cambridge on a scholarship, with a career as a mathematician ahead of him, he decided to be a 'pioneer in the land of Zion'. He was fired not only by the idea of Zionism but also by his love for Sarah Jofe, the daughter of Dr Hillel Jofe. As they used to joke in the family, 'Dr Herzl was the matchmaker of the family'. The truth is that Herzl and the Zionist congresses and meetings brought together circles of Zionists from Palestine and Europe. Many of the families knew each other and the younger generations met and fell in love. At the famous congress in Basle when the question of Uganda was painfully discussed (1903), Dr Hillel Jofe represented Eretz Israel, as did David Yellin, and Herbert Bentwich represented the English Zionist Organisation. The families continued to meet and visit each other and it resulted in the marriage of Joseph Bentwich to the daughter of Dr Jofe and of Thelma Bentwich to the son of David Yellin.

The Jofes lived in Zichron Ya'akov (the village established by and in honour of Baron Rothschild). When Nita and her husband Michael Lange came to visit the Jofes on their honeymoon in 1913, they fell in love with the place and she wrote home: 'I feel inclined to buy a mountain and try my luck!' The 'Carmel' mountain pulled the other members of the family with an irresistable attraction and they followed.

The name Carmel was always one of the family myths, the culmination of their dreams. It is repeated again and again in the names of the family: Carmelcourt in Kent, Carmel Court at Zichron, a daughter Carmel, and many a niece called Carmel. Of all the children, eight went to live permanently in Palestine, none of whom left. All of the girls were pretty and very talented. The only 'black sheep', as Rachel tells me, was her aunt Dorothy, who could not live up to the expectations of artistic aspiration on the one hand, and the restrictive Jewish observance on the other. She finally succumbed to the stress and became a convert to Christianity and lived out her life in a convent in the north of England. Her father 'sat *shiva*' and only her brother Joseph used to visit her from time to time. Her aunt Margery was the prettiest of all; nevertheless she never married. She was the constant companion of her father at all the later congresses and took care of him after the death of their mother in 1915. She went to live in Palestine with Herbert in 1927. They lived in Jerusalem.

The Bentwiches concentrated in two locations: at Carmel Court in Zichron, and at Alharizi Street in Rehavia, Jerusalem. Thelma and Eliezer Yellin built the first house in Rehavia, No. 1 Alharizi Street; Joseph's family lived at No. 6 and Herbert and Margery lived at No. 8.

The Bentwiches all had British passports, of course, and used to travel to England on vacation on British ships from

Haifa on which British soldiers used to sail for home leave. Because of their British citizenship, the Turks expelled them during World War I and they stayed in Britain. They left their Zichron estate for the duration and only returned in 1919. Norman Bentwich, who was later to be Attorney-General in the Mandate Administration, went to Palestine from service in Egypt with General Allenby's army.

Rachel recounts the story of her aunt Thelma who as a young musician fell in love with a non-Jew. Such a liaison was of course completely barred by Herbert. He also put a ban on her performing music on Shabbat – her life was full of these conflicts. One Yom Kippur, when the family was all ready to walk to synagogue, Thelma refused to join them. When they returned home, they found her in a state of nervous breakdown. After some medical treatment in London, she was sent to Israel to recuperate. She had a marvellous time there – the fresh mountain breeze, riding horses and camels – so in 1920 she fell in love with the land and also with the son of David Yellin, the friend of her father in Jerusalem. Again, Zionism proved to be the family matchmaker.

How did their sister Lilian reach America and not Zichron? This is a most beautiful story. When they were all still living in London in Avenue Road (we know the date precisely, it was in 1904), Herbert was awaiting the visit of a special emissary of the American Zionists, a young rabbi, Israel Friedlander, who worked in the Jewish Theological Seminary in New York. He was late, so Herbert asked Lilian, his eldest child, to wait outside and help the guest who had apparently lost his way. She saw not far from the house a young man holding his head in his hands and crying. She crossed the road and approached him: 'May I help you?', to which he answered: 'I am expected by the Bentwich family but I have just received a terrible message, that Dr Herzl has passed away!' and he continued to cry and could not control himself. Then and there, seeing a young man crying with so much sincere pain for the death of Herzl, she decided in her heart: this is the man I want to marry. In a few months they were married and their first-born son (1905) was named Herzl.

The story of Lilian, who had five more children born in America, has a tragic ending. Her husband, a first-rate Arabic scholar as well as a Judaic scholar, left in 1920 on a mission to the Ukraine, to bring relief money from the American Jewish Joint Distribution Committee. He was killed by robbers and his burial place is unknown; he left a widow with six children in New York. Herbert went to America to bring them first to London but with Carmel Court in Zichron in mind as their final destination. One of Lilian's children, Daniel, who was a child prodigy as a pianist in America, continued playing in Palestine. He later returned to New York to resume his studies at the Juilliard School, when one day he jumped from a high window, committing suicide. This was another terrible blow to the family but still not the last. Lilian established 'Beit Daniel' in his memory, a centre for music amid the tranquil natural scenery of Zichron Ya'akov.

Music at Beit Daniel, Zichron Ya'akov

Nita, the sixth daughter, was the pioneer at Zichron. She and her husband Michael Lange bought 'not the whole

mountain' but 77 dunam of it, a huge plot of rocky land on which they planted and built the Lange Estate. This was on the outskirts of Moshav Zichron Ya'akov and they made it a real 'English garden in Zion', a centre for the social and cultural life of the Yishuv. The beautiful house, with its flowers, goldfish pond and tennis court was the setting of many receptions, concerts and balls. Guests – among them Chaim Weizmann, the High Commissioner Herbert Samuel, Menahem Ussiskin, Henrietta Szold and others of the Mandate elite – used to arrive in carriages, and the entrance gate and stables are still to be seen today. They had the first telephone in the area with line no. 1. Today, this mansion is in ruins but has been declared a national protected site and is to be renovated. Rachel told me how they insisted on employing only Jewish workers (among them Rachel Yanait, later to become the wife of the second President of Israel, Itzhak Ben-

Rachel Shavit-Bentwich on the estate in Zichron Ya'akov showing the entrance used by the horse carriages in the 1920s

Zvi) and had comfortable quarters built for them. We toured the place and were upset to see the deplorable state of the buildings.

The avenue of palms and the whole grove of pine trees were planted by Nita and the rest of the Bentwiches. On a stone bench, in the shade of the pomegranate trees, there is an inscription, with the Hebrew dates, which reads:

> In memory of the beloved Michael Lange and Nita née Bentwich who planted this garden and this forest around their home.

Tragedy haunted them and struck again. Nita died suddenly at the age of 30. She succumbed to an infection after peritonitis when the only doctor in Zichron was attending another patient at a distance on that night. Michael Lange endeavoured to continue farming the model estate. He proposed in vain to Margery Bentwich; he could not bear the loneliness and three years after Nita's death shot himself when in deep depression.

The house of Muriel Bentwich where Rachel Shavit now lives and works is full of family memorabilia – pieces of inlaid Victorian furniture from the house in Avenue Road, and many old and fading photographs telling the story of all the generations of the Bentwiches.

Eretz Israel and, in particular, Mount Carmel acted as a magnet attracting all of them to realise their dream. As Lilian wrote to her father: 'And I shall plant them upon their Land, and they shall no more be pulled out of their Land' (Amos, IX, 15), a poignant expression of the sentiments that ran in the family.

Herbert Bentwich died on 25 June 1932 at his Rehavia home. Never overshadowed by the family tragedies, he never looked aside but only forward to his 'Pilgrimage to the Land of Promise'. He was a man of refined consciousness and of remarkable character. Like the patriarchs of old, he acquired an 'Ahusat Kever', a burial plot. The Bentwiches – Herbert, his wife Susie, whose remains he brought to Palestine with him, his son Norman and other members of the family are all buried in a beautiful private plot on the slopes of Mount Scopus overlooking the Temple Mount.

31

John M. Hignett as a child, in the garden of No. 58 in the 1930s

No. 58 in the 1930s

By 1932, the house on Avenue Road had fallen into disrepair and neglect. It needed a major overhaul and considerable work of rebuilding and restoration. The lease was bought in 1933 by the Hignett family, owners of a Liverpool tobacco factory which merged in due course with the Imperial Tobacco Company. Mr Reginald Hignett was a sculptor. His little statues of a frog and an owl still adorn our garden. In March 1934, John Hignett, their only son, was born in the room that serves today as the master bedroom. Through mutual friends, he once asked to visit the house in which he had been born and had spent the first five years of his life. The first thing he did after entering was to go straight to the corner of the garden where, under thick foliage he looked for the frog. 'Here it is', he exclaimed with joy! 'And here is the little hole where water used to come out'. And we had never even noticed the frog before, and didn't know that it was in the middle of what had once been a small pond.

In 1939, his father was mobilised, the rest of the family moved abroad, first to Bermuda then to Canada, never to return to live in Avenue Road. The house was locked and only the caretaker, Mr Briggs, lived in it. The house was damaged by a bomb in 1941 (many buildings in Swiss Cottage, Adelaide Road and Avenue Road suffered hits in the war). The house again went through substantial repairs and changes and in June 1947 it was sold to a certain Mr Woodford Ellis-Hill. On 16 January 1950 the property was 'transferred to Dr Mordecai Eliash of 18 Manchester Square' who was at the time Envoy Extraordinary and Minister Plenipotentiary of the Israeli Legation.

Thus, after a long interval and interruption, the Jewish presence returned to 58 Avenue Road and the circle 'was made whole'. The story of close ties with Zionism and Eretz Israel, which had started in St John's Wood with the Bentwich family, now continues in the same place with the Residence of the official representatives of the State of Israel. Sometimes I feel that Herbert Bentwich is looking on and smiling with satisfaction at the blue and white flag raised aloft over his old house.

Dr Mordecai Eliash: 'The homeless Minister'

In the *Evening Standard* of 14 October 1949 we read as follows:

> Dr M. Eliash, Israeli Minister, has housing worries. Until a month ago he lived in a hotel. Recently his 22-year-old daughter Rachel left her medical studies at the Hebrew University to join her father here. She becomes his First lady as he is a widower. Search for a permanent home for the Minister and his daughter by the officials of the Israeli Legation has been unsuccessful. For the last month they have been living in a rented house in St. John's Wood. But the owner returns from abroad in a few days. Unless *a house is found quickly*, Dr Eliash and his daughter will be homeless.

The story goes on that someone in the community remembered the house of the Bentwich family, and as it happened, it was on the market! Some of the leaders of the community, including Simon Marks, Israel Sieff (with great support from his wife, Rebecca), Harry Sacher – 'The Family' as they were known collectively – with Sigmund Gestetner and Rosser Chinn embarked on this project with great enthusiasm and fervour. Some people even claim to remember the sum of £5000 paid for the lease, or so I was told during my research. But there are no documents as it was all carried through with great love and discretion, and with respect for the newly-born State. It was to be the first official venue for the representatives of Israel, and it was a part of the general euphoria and emotional preparations to welcome them with the best that the Community could offer. Unfortunately, there was a sad end to the story of Israel's first emissary. Dr Eliash died suddenly on a Shabbat afternoon, the day before he was due to take up residence in Avenue Road.

Dr Mordecai Eliash was born in the Ukraine in 1892. He was a scholar and spoke 12 languages, among them Semitic. He enjoyed a long career in the legal world and became first President of the Jewish Bar Association in Great Britain. Later he was legal advisor to the Vaad Leumi – the 'government'

Bust of Dr Mordecai Eliash by Avram Melnikoff (Courtesy: Jewish Chronicle)

before the establishment of the State itself. He moved to the Jewish Agency desk at the United Nations in 1947 where in the following year he was succeeded by Abba Eban. It is an interesting matter to recall that on the staff of the Mission in New York in those days of 'the State in the making' were Arthur Lourie, Michael Comay, Dr Eliash, Gideon Rafael and Eliahu Elath, all of whom would be nominated subsequently as ambassadors to London.

Dr Eliash became the first Israeli Minister to the Court of St James only after 13 May 1949 when the British and Israeli governments simultaneously announced their agreement 'to raise the status of their legations'. He presented his credentials to King George VI, and his small staff at the legation were invited to the Palace Garden Party that summer.

He did not live to see the day when full *de jure* recognition was granted. He stayed for 11 months at an Orthodox Jewish hotel off Fitzjohns Avenue while 58 Avenue Road was being renovated. Being an observant Jew he would not move house on a Saturday but it was all planned for the next day, when he died. His body was actually brought there to lie in state until it was taken to the then small London airport at Croydon for burial in Israel. The King sent a message of condolence. Eliash was buried in Jerusalem, his funeral attended by Ben-Gurion, the Cabinet and thousands of Israelis. In London, Mr Reginald – Reggie – Kidron became the acting representative of the State until the arrival of Eliahu Elath who became the first Ambassador to reside at 58 Avenue Road.

It was Reggie Kidron who had the privilege of raising the flag for the first time on the Embassy offices at 18 Manchester Square. It is hard to describe the exultation that enveloped the thousands of Jews and non-Jews watching for the first time the hoisting of the blue and white flag. British Jewry celebrated by the thousand, singing and dancing in the square. Large crowds watched in amazement the changing of plaques on the building from 'Legation' to 'Embassy of Israel'. People gathered to see for themselves how an Israeli passport looked. Millions followed the news of the drama of the Jewish soldiers defending the newly born state. In the synagogue services, Chief Rabbi Israel Brodie added a special prayer for the welfare of the State of Israel.

Eliahu Elath: first Israeli Ambassador to the Court of St James, 1949–1959

At the desk of the newly established Embassy sat Eliahu Elath, a handsome figure with silvery hair and polished manners. He was one of Israel's first-generation diplomats and a leading Arabist. He served as a symbol of the good diplomat for the noviciacy of the newly established Foreign Office.

Born in the Ukraine in 1903, the son of Menachem and Rivka Epstein, he was arrested in his youth for Zionist activities and went to Palestine in 1925. He studied at the Hebrew University (later he was to become its President), and then at the University of Beirut, where he worked also as an undercover agent for the Jewish Agency. He served as Head of the Middle East Department of the Jewish Agency, then first Israeli Representative and Ambassador to the United States of America. He was appointed to London in 1950 in succession to Dr Eliash at a time when memories of the last unhappy days of the Mandate were still raw and British policy at the Foreign Office was still fundamentally pro-Arab.

His wife, Zehava, was born in Palestine in 1910, a graduate of a teachers' college in Jerusalem, a painter and sculptor, whose works were the first to adorn the new Embassy and private Residence.

Elath will always be remembered as the first representative of the 'State to be' in Washington, who, on 13 May 1948, sent a message by taxi to the White House, pointing out that the State for which Weizmann sought recognition would be called 'Israel'. On the same day, the recognition was sent in a letter by President Truman and addressed to Elath, and the announcement went on the air at once: 'The United States recognises the *de facto* authority of the new State of Israel'. At the same time the British High Commissioner, Sir Alan Cunningham, had sailed from Haifa on a cruiser with his last forces in Palestine.

After a few days back in Jerusalem, the Elaths were soon settling down in London at 58 Avenue Road. To be the first Ambassador in London after the bitterness of relations with Britain during the Mandate, to break the ice, the animosity, to try to build a new set of relations of trust and equal partner-

Sculpture by Mrs Elath

35

Ambassador Eliahu Elath ready to present his credentials at the Palace, 1950 (Courtesy: Jewish Chronicle)

ship, so close to the final days of the struggle for independence from British rule, was not an easy job, no enviable task. Even more to the point, he arrived in London during the Labour government of Prime Minister Attlee (1945–51) when Ernest Bevin was Secretary of State for Foreign Affairs. According to protocol, as a newly appointed envoy of State, Elath had to pay a visit to the Foreign Secretary and present him with a copy of his letters of credence to the Court of St James before presenting them to the King. This is a routine introductory visit, and it is not the occasion for political debate or the discussion of matters of state. But this is how Ambassador Elath remembers his first meeting with Bevin: 'He opened by saying that he was always opposed to the Balfour Declaration, and never believed that it would be possible to realise it. It was, in his opinion, "an injustice, and a terrible political declaration".' Then he stopped talking, and waited for the Ambassador to reply.

Elath had decided beforehand not to get involved in a heated debate at this first meeting, so he replied calmly that as the representative of the State of Israel he was not there to discuss the merits of the Balfour Declaration. It was his great privilege to represent the new State in Great Britain, the country which had fulfilled such an important and historic role in the creation of the State. He expressed his hope that he would get his Prime Minister's support to bring about positive relations between the two countries, based on trust and understanding. After a few moments of silence, Bevin suggested that Elath call on him whenever he needed to and wished him a successful stay in Britain for the benefit of both countries. Elath continues: 'I left him with a strong feeling that nothing had changed in his anti-Zionist attitude, even after the official recognition of Israel by Great Britain'.

Following the General Election of 1950, Labour held power under Attlee and although Bevin continued at the Foreign Office, he was already a sick man. Elath recounts in his memoirs his last meeting with Bevin before his death. Bevin wanted very much to find a solution to the Middle East conflict and, at the same time, to strengthen Britain's position in Egypt and the area as a whole. Sir William Strang, Permanent Under-Secretary of State at the Foreign Office, suggested that Elath invite Bevin for lunch at the Ambassador's residence for a private or rather a secret meeting. Elath recounts how he telephoned his wife about 'the very special guest coming to lunch' in their home. He wondered why it was so urgent and why at home and not at the office. His wife received a call from Bevin's physician who, knowing his patient's propensity to 'eat well', asked her for a very light meal, since rich food would be harmful to his condition.

They dined alone. Bevin asked Elath to go to Israel and relate their whole discussion directly to Ben-Gurion, not by cable or letter, but in person. He told him that the same mission was entrusted to the Egyptian Ambassador who had already left for Cairo. Bevin told Elath that he had decided to get involved and to secure the backing of both Governments because he saw in the Middle East a potential danger to the whole world. Israel's victory in the war of 1948–49 was not concluded with peace agreements and the situation would only remain in jeopardy and to the detriment of Israel's development and prosperity. The Arabs also could not devote their resources to a constructive future, and therefore he felt claims of responsibility to reach a peace treaty between Israel and Egypt, as a beginning of a more comprehensive peace for the whole of the Middle East – and he would be willing to act as mediator in the forthcoming negotiations. He saw Britain's important role in the area and he trusted in Ben-Gurion's wisdom to accept his proposal. As for the Arab side, he concluded by saying: 'I did a lot for the Arabs, so I expect them to accept my suggestion'.

It was Bevin's last effort to frame a role for the British presence in the Middle East, the swan song of someone who had been one of the worst political enemies of Zionism and the Yishuv during the final years of the struggle for the creation of the State and the establishment of Israel.

Elath's meeting with Churchill

While serving in the USA from 1945 to 1949, Elath heard a lot of praise for Churchill from Bernard Baruch, President Truman's Special Advisor. Baruch made the first contacts and gave Elath much advice before he assumed his post in London, as did President Weizmann when Elath went to bid farewell before leaving for London. 'Remember', the President told the Ambassador, 'one day all those in opposition will again be great and important'. Elath reminisces:

> I arrived in London in the summer of 1949, to represent the State of Israel in the capital, where the 'historic declaration of a National Home for the Jewish people in Eretz Israel' was given. I wrote to Mr Churchill and asked to be received, to bring him regards from his friends in Washington and Rehovot. I was invited to meet him on 15 September, at his home near Hyde Park. I found Churchill in his bedroom on the second floor, in his pyjamas and in bed, reading a book while a little black kitten lay at his feet. Years later, his doctor Lord Moran told me that Churchill was at that time

recovering from a stroke but that was being kept secret, and he was under doctor's orders to spend half his day in bed. This, therefore, was a special gesture and a compliment to be received in his bedroom.

Churchill congratulated me on my appointment to London, and said that the establishment of the State of Israel was one of the major events in the history of the world, and that he was proud of his contribution as a 'Zionist all his life'. He expressed concern that Bevin would obscure or detract from the wonderful image of Balfour and the role of Britain in promoting the National Home of the Jewish people.

After a short pause, he continued to say that Israel had no better friend than the British people who were realistic and romantic at the same time. They admired the courage and the rights of the Jewish people on the one hand, and the moral qualities of 'the people of the Bible' on the other. He continued by analysing the world political situation, the Cold War, and Stalin's position, and concluded by saying in a firm voice that Israel had to be a strong state in order to defend democracy.

He showed interest in the development projects in agriculture, conquest of the desert, industry, and mentioned with pride his relations with the brilliant scientist Dr Chaim Weizmann: 'God blessed the Jewish people, that at such a time in their history, He has sent them such an outstanding statesman and scientist as Dr Weizmann'.

The conversation lasted more than an hour, and it was of course dominated by Churchill. I left with the deep feeling that we had in Churchill one of the best and strongest friends of Zionism and of the State of Israel. This was proved when, on the 26th October 1951, Churchill and his party came back to power. He continued to be that voice in Parliament defending the needs of Israel and praising the young country on many occasions.

Thus Ambassador Elath was able throughout his long years in London to enjoy, after the bitterness of Bevin's displeasure, the appreciation, support and friendship of Churchill and his government.

The Second Ambassador, Arthur Lourie and Mrs Jeannete Lourie, 1960–1965

Born in Johannesburg, South Africa in 1903, Arthur Lourie joined the group of hard-working Zionists devoted to Chaim Weizmann and the Jewish Agency at their London head-quarters (77 Great Russell Street) in the 1930s. At that time the Zionist idea was still '90 per cent fantasy and ten per cent reality'. In 1933 he became the political secretary of the Agency. He was later a delegate to the UN Conference in San Francisco (1945) and became Israel's first Consul-General in New York in 1948. Whenever he went to his office he would see clusters of Jews assembled at the front of the building, clicking away with cameras trying to 'take in' the wonder of the 'State' or look at the first Israeli passports which in those days were printed in French and Hebrew 'punishing the English' for the behaviour of Ernest Bevin.

At that time in London, Winston Churchill became the great British voice in support of Zionism. In a fierce debate in Parliament he said: 'Whether the Rt. Hon. Gentleman likes it or not, the coming into being of a Jewish State in Palestine is an event in world history to be viewed in the perspective not of a generation or a century but in the perspective of a thousand, two thousand or even three thousand years!' It is worth repeating and reminding ourselves of these words of this great friend of the Jewish people.

Arthur Lourie, a close aide of Abba Eban, replaced him at the UN when Eban was appointed Ambassador to Washington. From 1957 to 1960, Lourie served as Ambassador to Canada. He and his wife Jeanette (née Leibel) reached London in 1960.

The 1960s, the years of Ambassador Lourie's tour of duty, can be counted as the years of the peace enjoyed by Israel between the withdrawal from Sinai and Gaza in 1957 and the Six Day War of 1967. These years consolidated the internal as

Ambassador Arthur Lourie ready to present his credentials at the Palace, 1950 (Courtesy: Jewish Chronicle)

well as external strengths of the army, the economy, and the international standing of the country and saw Israel continuing to absorb a steady stream of immigrants. Relations between Britain and the Middle East continued to be constrained by Britain's economic interests among the Arab states. Nevertheless, Britain began to see in Israel a positive influence in the region, one that could contain the Nasserite threat of expansion. Gradually, a remarkable improvement in relations grew between Britain and Israel, the change building on the outcome of some crucial visits. Firstly, Defence Minister Shimon Peres met the British Minister of State for Foreign Affairs, John Profumo, early in March 1960. This was followed by a very significant meeting between Prime Ministers David Ben-Gurion and Harold Macmillan on 17 March 1960. Ambassador Lourie was active in promoting

Harold Macmillan greeting David Ben-Gurion, 1961, with Arthur Lourie (Courtesy: Jewish Chronicle)

both these encounters when Ben-Gurion was on his way back from his historic meeting in Washington with President Eisenhower. In his first statement on arrival in London Ben-Gurion said:

> It is with a sense of deep satisfaction that I can set foot on British soil. I am very happy that recent years have seen a growing mutual understanding and cordiality in the relations between our two countries... We shall always recall with profound

42

gratitude Britain's contribution in the first stages of our national regeneration in our homeland. The people of Israel share with the people of Britain devotion to democratic values, to freedom, to peace.

Then followed a lengthy meeting between the two leaders at Downing Street in which they discussed the global situation as well as the Middle East. Of interest is a subject raised by Ben-Gurion concerning membership of the Commonwealth which he had already put on record in a meeting with General Brian Robertson, Commander of British Forces in the Middle East, in 1951:

> I am ready to make that offer again and to aim at the establishment of the same intimate and friendly relations between Israel and Britain, as if Israel were in fact a member of the Commonwealth.

He was convinced that the two countries shared the same interests to an extent that could justify such an arrangement. In the light of recent offers made to Israel by the Secretary-General of the Commonwealth concerning the possibility of 'joining the club' this echo has a historic ring.

Ambassador and Mrs Lourie with Richard Crossman, the Foreign Secretary, at their farewell dinner, 1965 (Courtesy: Jewish Chronicle)

43

It was during Ambassador Lourie's time that Britain agreed to sell Israel 60 additional Centurion tanks on top of the 30 supplied in 1959.

During their stay, the house had the atmosphere of a 'real ambassadorial establishment'. Waiters in white jackets and gloves were employed by Mrs Lourie to serve guests. Many politicians and intellectuals of British society were entertained. Mrs Lourie made improvements to the house despite a tight budget by introducing modern central heating (replacing the old fireplaces) and extending the large reception room used for the largest gatherings. In Israel, those were the times of greatest austerity and whenever the Foreign Office could not allocate money for certain expenses, the Louries themselves paid. They brought to the residence their own silver coffee set and china.

AT THIS POINT, I should like to depart from my narrative to make a private observation on looking into the inventory of the Residence. One can read between the lines and note the changing character of the house as ambassadors succeeded each other. The first three ambassadors were 'spoiled' by the Jewish community and the Residence was lavished with gifts, beautiful furniture or pieces of silver. There is a long list of these treasures but I should like to highlight the following:
- a set of George III antique silver salt cellars, the gift of Lord and Lady Marks of Broughton;
- a gold upholstered Victorian armchair, the gift of Mrs H. Gestetner;
- a Regency sideboard, the gift of Mrs H. Sacher;
- two tall gold-brocade side chairs, the gift of Mrs H. Morrison;
- a William and Mary cabinet, drop-leaf desk, also the gift of Mrs Gestetner;
- an oak table, the gift of Mrs Flora Solomon;
and it goes on and on.

This atmosphere changed completely with the arrival in June 1965 of Aharon Remez. His predecessors had been feted by the community and they were ushered into British society

with the expectation of the panoply of traditional ambassadorial style. He and his wife felt rather that the Residence
should reflect Israeli style.

There is a long correspondence in the Embassy archive
between Mrs Remez and Jerusalem regarding her request to
purchase items of crafts and art from Israel. She wanted a
small rug made by Maskit (the Israeli company employing
immigrant artists in order to preserve the folklore of their
different communities of origin). The Office claimed that it
would be too expensive but she had set her heart on it and
insisted and finally secured it for the Residence.

The same thing happened over some pictures by Lotan and
other Israeli painters. She insisted on adorning the house, less
with silver and antiques, but more with ceramics from Israel
and the olive wood typical of Israeli crafts. There is another
lengthy exchange of letters regarding the purchase of a piano.
Ambassador Remez writes quite explicitly that there is a
possibility of 'receiving a piano as a gift' but it is not 'right or
respectable to do so and I am not ready to get gifts like these'.
In the end, they received permission and an allocation to buy
a 'restored piano'. They purchased a Bechstein Grand of 1904
'that costs new 1753 guineas – but second-hand, with
guarantee, will cost us only 450 guineas, no doubt it is a
bargain!', writes the Ambassador to the officials in Jerusalem.
And what a fine bargain it has proved. We still have it today,
tuned to concert pitch providing great service and pleasure.

The first set of china with the emblem of the State of Israel
also arrived at the house during Ambassador and Mrs Remez's
time. Subsequently, negotiations started between the
Embassy and the Israeli museums to secure the loan of Israeli
works of art for display at the Residence. In Ambassador
Rafael's time, in 1974, the Israel Museum loaned works from
the collection of Mrs Charlotte Bergman. When the Museum
requested their return in 1978 for an exhibition by Mrs
Bergman, Ambassador Kidron returned them but opened
negotiation for four other works to replace them. By the time
of our arrival, I decided to 'negotiate' directly with Israeli
artists themselves who are thrilled to have the opportunity to
have their works displayed so splendidly in a house visited by
hundreds of people and representing the cultural life of Israel.

Sidney Harris

Some of the valuable furniture in the Residence

Throughout the years, the Residence has accumulated its own collection of paintings, mainly by Israeli artists, like Pima, Anna Ticho, Rubin, Ardon, Shaar and Avniel. After all, Israel's musicians or artists, like its writers, reflecting the cultural life of their country, are its best ambassadors!

The first sabra Ambassador – Aharon Remez and Mrs Rita Remez, 1965–1970

'An Ambassador enjoys his job, its variety, its freedom from routine, the opportunity to meet every class of people in the country', writes Aharon Remez at the end of his tour of duty in the UK, 'his schedule may change, there is no typical working day'. He continues:

> Unpredictable events occur every day. He may spend a whole morning in Whitehall, in Parliament or at the Foreign Office, or at the Embassy, then a long line of national days at other embassies. He starts his day with working breakfasts followed by lunches, cocktails; he gives lectures, visits other cities, the universities, Jewish communal bodies; there is correspondence, cables from Jerusalem.

These reflections of Ambassador Remez hold true for all.

Aharon Remez, air force officer and commander, diplomat, politican, artist, was born in Tel Aviv in 1919. He was Israel's Ambassador to Britain from 1965 to 1970. He died in Jerusalem on 3 April 1994.

The son of David Remez, one of Israel's pioneering founding fathers, he was a member of Kibbutz Kfar Blum and became an RAF pilot in World War II like his contemporary, Ezer Weizman. Later he put air force flair and discipline to good effect in the embryonic Israeli air force in 1948 when he became its commander (1948–51). Then he became head of Israel's Purchasing Mission in the USA (1951–53) before returning home to fill various important offices. He entered politics on the Mapai list (the Israel Labour Party, as it was then known) in 1956 but resigned from the Knesset after two years complaining that he felt he was 'wasting his time'. He became Director of the Solel-Boneh, the Histadrut Building

Ambassador Remez addressing the Israel at Selfridges Exhibition, 1965 (Courtesy: Jewish Chronicle)

Company, then administrator at the Weizman Institute. Later, he took up a senior position at the Foreign Ministry and was subsequently appointed Ambassador to Britain in 1965.

He enjoyed the many facets of life in London. He was a skilful and colourful diplomat. He was used to working with people and words, but his activities in retirement show him to have been a man of many parts and complexity: he took up carpentry, painting and sculpture, using wood and plastic mainly. It was quite a change to work in solitude and to deal with materials, but the breadth of talents shows the rounded man.

His time in London coincided with those most dramatic days before and after the Six Day War. Events moved rapidly, and in London on the television everything in Israel under the threat of war looked terrifying, unreal. On 19 May, President Shazar stopped at Heathrow en route to the Israel pavilion at Expo 67 in Canada. Ambassador Remez and his staff were at the airport to welcome him but the atmosphere was fraught with anxieties.

All in Britain were concerned. The Residence received hundreds of calls, people were frustrated, worried, some even hysterical. The culminating moment for staff here in London, far from the everyday reality of Israel, was the interview with King Ibn Saud at Claridges which was witnessed on television by millions. He stated that the only solution to the crisis was 'the extermination of the State of Israel' – his words bringing to mind the Nazi 'final solution'. It triggered reactions and an eruption of emotion and massive support for the tiny state in its danger. There was as yet no Israeli television and the cries of '*Jihad*' from the Arab networks exposed the isolation of Israel and its impending fate which gave rise to an indescribable change in Britain.

Overnight, the Ambassador and his staff found themselves engulfed by the love and support, not only of the Jewish community but of the country at large. The following are examples of the sentiments of those days. The Christian Society for the Distribution of Holy Scriptures wrote to the Embassy: 'On behalf of the Council of the Society and the many Christian people we represent, we desire to express sympathy in this day of crisis and to assure you of our prayers on behalf of Israel . . .'. A nurse, like so many others, wrote: 'I am not a Jew but an Irish Roman Catholic and feel you need all the help you can get ... would you kindly forward my name and address to the department concerned with volunteers ...'. From another letter: 'I feel strongly about Israel to do something to help, namely by working in Israel. Since I have an agricultural education and experience of poultry farming, I could be of some use in this field ...'.

Mrs Remez recalls with excitement how moved she was at one event during the weeks preceding the Six Day War. She was hosting a tea for WIZO and the ladies present suddenly started taking off their pearls and offering them as donations towards the approaching war.

There were many moving letters from people ready to help, to receive evacuee children, to contribute whatever they could. Some taxi-drivers, many of them Jewish, insisted on donating a day's proceeds, all in pennies and shillings. The Residence became the centre for the concerns of so many, from Israeli students to journalists, show people and many others. And after the victory, the sensation was overwhelming – a sharp change from the sense of danger to the euphoria of relief and joy. The Residence was flooded with flowers and calls from friends. It was also a moment of spiritual metamorphosis for many in the Jewish community who now felt a part of the people, found their identity and common bonds. All this was reflected in the daily life of the representatives of Israel in the house.

Recently, I enjoyed a long conversation with Mrs Remez in Jerusalem. She lives in the leafy neighbourhood of St Simon, surrounded by little sculptures and other works of her late husband. She reminisces about London and has fond memories of the time and their friends there. He was not only the first 'sabra' Ambassador but also the first with a family of young children to be installed at 58 Avenue Road. The garden had its first playground where their daughters, aged three, ten and twelve used to invite their friends from school to play.

Dr Alec Lerner mentioned at the time that it reminded him of the White House in the days of the Kennedys, when the

Mr and Mrs Elath with Dr and Mrs Alec Lerner in 1962 (Courtesy: Jewish Chronicle)

house was occupied by a family with young children, noise and toys everywhere. At the Remez's first reception at the Residence to honour Mr Elath in his new role as President of the Hebrew University, the three-year-old girl came down dressed in her ballet costume to stand in line to receive the guests.

Ambassador Remez started making sculptures in wood, of which the first were busts. One of these pieces stood on the mantleshelf in the dining room. Teddy Kollek came to London to launch the Jerusalem Foundation and there was a lunch in his honour. Among the guests, he remembers Yehudi Menuhin, Laurence Olivier and Henry Moore, who noticed the sculpture and examined it closely. He recommended moving it to a better position and varnishing it for its protection. Mrs Remez still remembers their excitement and satisfaction that an artist like Henry Moore would notice and take an interest in the first work of an aspiring sculptor.

In those days there were not yet guards or security men, Israeli or British. Only when Ben-Gurion or Golda Meir came for an overnight stay would a policeman drop by to check the house and the well-being of the important guests. She actually remembered the purpose of a visit Ben-Gurion made to London (at a time when he was not Prime Minister) when he came for a secret meeting with Musa El-Alami, one of the leading Palestinians and a remarkable and cultured man, a respected headmaster of a well-known college, a man of peace and moderation. Late in the evening, Ambassador Remez sent Rita round to their neighbours, Teddy and Lois Sieff, to ask them to act as hosts next day at a confidential lunch. Ben-Gurion, in disguise, crossed the street and met Musa El-Alami in the Sieff home for lengthy talks.

Mrs Remez recalls with great affection their driver, Alec Gee. He was the Ambassador's driver for many years, a fine and very special person. After the driver had worked for 18 years at the Embassy, Ambassador Remez decided it was time for Mr Gee to go on a visit to Israel as the guest of the Israeli Foreign Service. He organised this to the delight not only of Mr Gee but also of all those who had known him over the years. Much later, when he went for the second time, he contacted the Remez family and paid them a visit and their friendship lasted until his death.

Ambassador Michael Comay and Mrs Joan Comay, 1970–1973

Born in 1908 in South Africa, Michael Comay was married to Joan Comay, a writer and historian, and one of the editors of the *Encyclopaedia Judaica*. Formerly high-ranking in the South African army, he was among the founders of Israel's diplomatic corps. He became his country's first Ambassador to Canada, then head of the Permanent Mission to the UN. He became Ambassador to Britain in 1970. Michael Comay had a great fondness for Britain and felt the appointment to London was the high point of his career. After Ambassador and Mrs Remez, the Comays restored formality to the Residence, insisting for instance on black ties at dinners.

Cordial relations with Britain became strained towards the

end of his tour of duty. He felt that the arms embargo imposed on the participants in the Yom Kippur War was unfair to Israel: 'Tanks were sold to us for defence, but spare parts were denied when we had to defend ourselves'. It fell to him to protest at Britain's policy of refusal to sell arms during the Yom Kippur War. He said time and again that the people of Israel felt let down by Britain at a crucial moment in their history. During the darkest days of the War, Ambassador Comay participated in a 'solidarity rally' in Trafalgar Square attended by an estimated crowd of 20,000 people including many non-Jews. He declared: 'The leaders who gave orders to march on Israel are war criminals. They must accept the responsibility for all the dead and maimed, for the waste of life and resources in this war'.

Ambassador Michael Comay speaking at the Royal Albert Hall on Israel's twenty-fifth Anniversary, 1973 (Courtesy: Jewish Chronicle)

Gentiles joined Jews in contributing to fund-raising for Israel. El-Al was besieged by volunteers, some waited for days for a flight on the few planes available. Thousands queued to give blood! Jews and non-Jews queued at St John's Wood Synagogue which came to resemble a casualty station. Among the blood-donors were three Egyptians who had once received assistance from Magen David Adom in Israel and wanted to help. A thousand pints of blood donated in London reached Israeli hospitals.

Comay's term in London ended under the cloud of the war and its aftermath. Days and nights of worry engulfed the Embassy and the Residence which followed with pain and anxiety every scrap of news from the battlefront, and welcomed with relief any positive turn of events. At that time, life at the Residence and the Embassy was also marred by the activities of a group of terrorists, the 'Black September', which subjected diplomats (and prominent Jewish figures) to a campaign of letter bombs. Police guards took up a high-profile stance at the gates.

Comay was a man of liberal thought, warning against the continued occupation of West Bank and Gaza, and of the debilitation of the moral and democratic character of Israel.

A lecture room has been established in his memory at the Rubin Academy of Music where he became chairman of the Board of Governors following his return from London and retirement.

Ambassador Gideon Rafael ready to present his credentials at the Palace, 1973 (Courtesy: Jewish Chronicle)

Ambassador Gideon Rafael and Mrs Nurit Rafael, 1973–1977

The day of Gideon Rafael's arrival in London, in December 1973, was one of unprecedented security at Heathrow. The first call the new Ambassador and his wife paid, straight from the airport and before going to the Residence, was to the hospital bedside of Edward Sieff who had been attacked by terrorists only a few days before. The atmosphere was especially tense after the attackers were caught with in their hands a list of more prominent figures to be targetted. Edward Sieff, who lived in Queen's Grove, around the corner from the Residence, was just out of the intensive care unit. His wife Lois received the new Ambassador and his wife and a strong bond formed between them. Years later, in 1994, the Embassy as well as Balfour House were the targets of renewed terrorist bombs. It evoked the memory that Israelis and the Jewish community are together as one as the target of fanatical terrorists.

Gideon Rafael, born in Germany in 1913 and educated at Berlin University, went to Palestine in 1934. He was among the founders of Kibbutz Hazorea. He represented the Haganah in Europe and was a member of the delegation of the Jewish Agency at the UN in 1947. Subsequently, he served the State in various capacities. He was among the first members of the Foreign Office staff under Moshe Sharett. In 1967, he was a permanent representative at the UN in one of the most dramatic periods in its annals.

Israelis now divide their lives into what happened before and after October 1973. The war which Israeli intelligence experts had defined as of 'low probability' erupted as a surprise and came as a terrible shock. In spite of the initial sense of doom, however, Israeli military superiority eventually won the day. On 25 October it was virtually all over. We all had to face the emotions of a tormented society and paid a high cost in casualties for the triumph. Great Britain and other European countries gave in to the threat of the cut in oil supply from the Arab regions. The decision of the Heath Government to deny the Israelis spare parts came as another harsh blow, while the USA started the famous airlift of

Ambassador and Mrs Rafael with Prime Minister Harold Wilson, 1976

supplies. It was only with the return of a Labour Government (under Harold Wilson) that the scars began to heal.

It is against this background that Ambassador Rafael came to his post. He had to operate in the aftermath of the Yom Kippur War at a time of oil crises and a diplomatic rift. These were sombre and hard times. Anglo-Israeli relations were soured by the embargo.

The change in government (from Heath to Wilson during the course of 1974) certainly brought a new sense of purpose and enthusiasm. Israel found old and new friends in the incoming administration. Prime Minister Yitzak Rabin, Foreign Minister Yigal Allon and Golda Meir were all invited on official visits which culminated in the visit of President Katzir in 1976, who was warmly received by Her Majesty and the Government. There was a change in substance as well as atmosphere in Anglo-Israeli relations.

During this time, relations were also established with Ireland and Ambassador Rafael duly presented his credentials in Dublin too. He and his successors served in this way until 1994 when full recognition and exchange of ambassadors were established between Ireland and Israel in their own right.

The Rafaels struck up many friendships, among them a warm relationship with Lord and Lady Avon (Churchill's niece) who invited them to their manor amid the Wiltshire downs. They reciprocated by inviting the Edens to the Residence. Conversation often ran back to the summer of 1956 and the Suez affair, both men having played influential roles at the time.

Ambassador Rafael constantly sought to develop and deepen relations not only with politicians but also in business and commercial circles in the UK. He also visited Jewish communities throughout the country, considering himself, like all ambassadors, accredited not only to the State but to Jewry at large.

One special event during their term was a party given in honour of Galina and Valeriy Panov, the Russian ballet dancers whose emigration to Israel stirred great emotion. The party was attended by many artists, public figures from the theatre, politics and the Jewish community.

Mrs Nurit Rafael pursued her professional activities in the field of education while serving in London. She was particularly involved with retarded children and those with special needs. She and the Ambassador constantly sought to present Israel and its artistic life, sponsoring concerts, art displays and musical evenings at the Residence which became an open house in their time for visiting Israelis, students, musicians, sporting figures, as well as politicians, Jews and Arabs alike. Arriving as they did at so critical a time, the Rafaels played an invaluable role in the restoration of confidence and fortitude among Israel's Jewish and non-Jewish supporters.

Ambassador Avraham Kidron and Mrs Shoshana Kidron, 1977–1979

We first knew and enjoyed the friendship of Avraham and Shoshana Kidron in London in 1959 where he was a popular First Secretary and Press Attaché (at only 37). A handsome couple, red-haired, young and elegant, their home was a meeting place for intellectuals, journalists, artists and Israelis on sabbatical. His low-key style enabled him to conduct the toughest of negotiations with calm and patience.

Born in Germany in 1920, he went to Palestine in 1934 in one of the first Youth Aliyah groups. He studied history and

56

political science at the Hebrew University. During the War of Independence, he served as Chief of Intelligence of the Haganah in Haifa. He was transferred to the Foreign Office in 1949, and then held various diplomatic posts in Rome, in Cyprus, in Yugoslavia as Minister, and as Ambassador first in the Phillipines, then in The Netherlands. In 1973, he returned to Jerusalem to become Director-General of the Foreign Office.

In July 1977, he presented his credentials to the Queen and in October of that year, to the President of the Irish Republic. He served as Ambassador in London only until 1979, one of the shortest terms in the house, when he was nominated Ambassador to Canberra. 'His early departure is no reflection on his standing in London' it was expressed at the time in some of the newspapers. Rather, it was an open secret that his transfer was a result of the changes in the civil service after the change of government in Israel in 1977.

Ambassador Avraham Kidron ready to present his credentials at the Palace, 1977

Ambassador Kidron's task in London proved difficult. He had to represent the new Prime Minister Menahem Begin who had been commander of the Irgun during the period preceding the establishment of the State of Israel. Although Israel's civil servants are not nominated or affiliated through the political system, and Ambassador Kidron was never associated with any of the parties, nonetheless his record is as one of the commanders of the Haganah.

In his last months in London, his main preoccupation was to ensure that relations between the two countries would not be adversely affected by the changes in government following the elections of 1977 in Israel and of 1979 in Britain. He prepared the ground for an unprecedented rapport between Callaghan and Begin, securing an invitation for Begin to visit Britain, the first Israeli Prime Minister to make a State Visit to London.

When Mr Begin arrived in London in June 1979, it was, however, Mrs Thatcher who hosted the luncheon at Downing Street. During the course of the speeches, Mr Begin reaffirmed the friendship between the two countries which 'are ready to pursue together peace and liberty in our region'. Mr Begin also paid tribute to Mrs Thatcher as 'a true friend of Israel and of the Jewish people'. She accepted in principle an invitation to visit Israel in her turn.

Ambassador Kidron celebrating Israel's Peace Treaty with Egypt, 1979, with (left to right) Eric Moonman, John Pardoe, Harold Wilson, Abba Eban and Trevor Chinn

In July 1979, Mrs Thatcher also gave a farewell luncheon to the Kidrons and they were guests of Douglas Hurd, Minister of State in charge of Middle Eastern Affairs at the Foreign Office, where he praised Ambassador Kidron and his excellent achievements during his tour. Harold Wilson also said goodbye to the Kidrons at a well-attended gathering at his home.

Prime Minister Begin and Ambassador Kidron at a Press Conference, 1979

58

Every Ambassador, as I have tried to make clear, brings individuality to his work and reveals aspects of his personality in action. Kidron's style was cool, quiet and confident. He held his listener's respect; he argued with sincerity and deployed a healthy sense of humour which was famous. Ambassador Kidron died suddenly in October 1982 in Canberra. He was aged 63, a senior diplomat, an honest and devoted ambassador of great abilities. His body was flown to Israel for burial in Jerusalem.

An ambassador in the front line: Ambassador Shlomo Argov and Mrs Hava Argov, 1979–1982

Shlomo Argov was born in Jerusalem in 1929, a seventh-generation Israeli with deep roots in the life of his country. Like many of his generation he was a member of the Palmach. He studied at Georgetown University in Washington, DC. Many years later, when serving as Minister and Deputy Ambassador at the Embassy in Washington, he would recall how, as a student, he worked for his living as a night-guard at the Embassy. He took an MA at the LSE. He was posted successively to Nigeria, Ghana and New York, later as Minister in Washington; then as Ambassador to Mexico, to the Netherlands and in 1979 to London.

Greville Janner MP, President of the Board of Deputies, greeting the Argovs on their arrival, 1979

Ambassador Shlomo Argov ready to present his credentials at the Palace, 1979

Shlomo Argov has become a symbol of the Israeli diplomat who not only fights for his country in the conventional forms of statesmanship but also faces the dangers of the frontline soldier exposed among the foremost. His mission in London was ended abruptly in tragic circumstances on 3 June 1982. Leaving the annual dinner of the De La Rue Company at the Dorchester (a men-only affair) he was shot before entering his car by two Arab terrorists. The assailants shot Mr Argov through the head using a semi-automatic submachine gun. Pursued into neighbouring streets, they also shot and seriously wounded the police security guard. The Ambassador and the policeman were taken first to Westminster Hospital, then moved to the National Hospital.

The attack caused revulsion and outrage not only in Israel but even more so among the general public in Britain. Mrs Thatcher, the Prime Minister, and Foreign Secretary Francis Pym sent personal messages to Prime Minister Begin and Mr Shamir, Foreign Minister at the time, as well as to the Argov family. The Queen also sent messages of sympathy. All the major Jewish bodies issued statements of outrage. Greville Janner, President of the Board of Deputies, summed up these feelings of 'shock, disbelief, disgust and horror'.

Hava Argov recalled in an interview in 1992, ten years later:

> On that night of the shooting, I stayed home at the residence, it being a men-only occasion. Around the time when I thought he should be coming home, I began to be rather nervous. Then the bell rang and the policeman said: 'Mrs Argov, I am sorry, your husband was shot!' It was in the back of my mind that something like this could happen. It still was an incredible shock. When I got to the hospital some of our friends were there already. One was praying. They took my husband into surgery. We just sat and waited. They did not know whether he was going to survive.

A few days after the shooting, the war started in Lebanon which many thought had been triggered by the attempt on Argov's life. He did not like to make the connection between what had happened to him and that terrible war where so many young boys were killed.

The community was in distress and 5000 people filled the Albert Hall on 13 June at a rally where Yoav Biran spoke, acting as Chargé d'Affaires. He recalls today:

> They wanted me to talk about Shlomo, it was so difficult! How can you do this about a person so close to you? There was a danger that it would

Yoav Biran and the Argov family at the Rally at the Albert Hall, June 1982

sound like an obituary. I did it as if I were talking to him, saying that we could not allow the terrorists to succeed. I think he would have appreciated it had he been there. He was a preacher who practised what he preached. He was a fighter and his struggle for life symbolised the national struggle.

The most sustained applause was for Gideon, Argov's son, who said: 'We have all been deeply touched and strengthened by this community reaction. Your message of support has eased the pain of the last ten days.'

On 16 July there were reports in the newspapers ... Argov able to speak, he recovered consciousness ... slight improvement ... and every week after, more reports of improvement bringing some rays of hope. Norman Grant, the neuro-surgeon who operated on Argov, announced: 'His conditions are better than expected. There is a possibility to transfer him to Israel.' On 30 July, Professor Beller, the leading Israeli neuro-surgeon came to London to visit the Ambassador for a full report on his situation. On 13 August, Argov went back to Israel accompanied by his family and Professor Beller. On his arrival at Hadassa, he managed to smile and said: 'I am sure with so many friends around me, I shall get better.'

In August 1984, after a long trial, the three Arab terrorists were sentenced, one for 35 years, the other two for 30 years for the attempted murder of Ambassador Argov. Scotland Yard, investigating the mass of documents found in the homes of the terrorists, discovered a 'hit list' of political and commercial Israeli-Jewish targets in London. Since that time, the Residence has been under police guard night and day and restrictions on the ambassadors' movements have been very strict.

In November 1985, Argov made a visit in his wheelchair to his colleagues at the Ministry in Jerusalem. He received a warm and rousing welcome.

Shlomo Argov is now in a rehabilitation unit at Hadassa. It has been a terrible tragedy. For more than 15 years now, the Hadassa Hospital on Mount Scopus has been his home. It is the only place where he can be cared for. He sits in a wheelchair. He is paralysed from the neck down and can only move his head and he needs to be nursed 24 hours a day. His situation is deteriorating and his eyesight is bad. His speech has become more and more difficult to understand. It is painful to watch Shlomo in this situation, Shlomo who was so eloquent and such an effective diplomat.

For Hava Argov, the 15 years have been a sad and lonely struggle to lead a normal life, to keep her family together. She still remains the classic ambassadorial wife, composed and calm. She and her children are undoubtedly as much Abu Nidal's victims as Shlomo Argov. We met in her small new apartment in Bayit Vegan. It is a protected building because she resides alone. Shlomo Argov is brought home only for a few hours each weekend and all the arrangements for a wheelchair have been made.

After all these years of suffering, Hava is still a very controlled and dignified lady. She told me that her feelings for London have not changed. They love London for here is where they first met – he as a student and she as a secretary at the Embassy; their courtship and their marriage took place in this city; for their honeymoon they toured Scotland. Thus Britain for them is a second home. But she cannot bear the thought of visiting their old home in Avenue Road or the Embassy offices in Kensington – it would be too painful and hurtful.

She recalls life in the Residence with great affection. They had a large and beautiful labrador which accompanied them loyally everywhere on their postings abroad (Mexico, USA, Holland). In London, they had to go through the separation of six months' quarantine. Finally, before they left London they had to put the big old dog to sleep.

She also remembers the first visit of the Egyptian Ambassador to the Residence when he attended the vin d'honneur on Independence Day, 1979. They shook hands and he said: 'Madame, I was a General in the Egyptian Army, now I am a soldier for peace!' She was brought to the verge of tears in the excitement of the occasion.

They used to travel alone during weekends, Shlomo at the wheel. One of their daughters was living with them. They loved Wales, they loved the countryside. They used to spend nights with friends watching documentary films from Israel. Like other ambassadors, they held concerts at the Residence. Georg Solti, famous conductor and neighbour, often used to join them for these musical evenings. Life at the Residence was exciting but peaceful until those dreadful shots in the night cut off the life of the family and cut short a brilliant diplomatic career.

Many endowments have been named in tribute to Argov. In 1983, he was honoured by the LSE when nominated one of their Honorary Fellows. Mrs Thatcher expressed her support for the fight against terrorism when she addressed a dinner in London at which two chairs were established in the name of Shlomo Argov at Bar-Ilan University and the Hebrew University. The British Friends of Hadassa Medical Relief Association unveiled a plaque in his honour at the

Neurosurgical Unit where Shlomo Argov receives treatment. Mrs Irene Sala, then President of the Association, said that the best way to show the community's affection for the Ambassador was to raise the funds needed for this vital unit.

London holds for the Argovs a bitter-sweet place in their life; it was where they first met, but it is also the place where their life together took such a tragic turn.

From Manchester to the Palace: Ambassador Yehuda Avner and Mrs Mimi Avner, 1983–1988

'Born in Manchester but given birth in Jerusalem': these are the words Yehuda Avner uses to define his Anglo-Jewish roots. 'In all my years on the throne', the Queen told him, 'I have never before received the credentials of a foreign ambassador who had been born in Britain!'

Born in Manchester, known to his English friends in Bnei Akiva as Gubby Haffner, Yehuda Avner went to Palestine alone in 1947. He remembers how he set off from Victoria Station and reached Haifa on 'that ecstatic night just before the UN resolution brought Israel into being'. He recalls with amusement how the British arrested him for carrying weapons for the Haganah and being taken to a British officer who recognised him immediately from their schooldays in Manchester.

Other memories are more sombre. Fighting with his unit under the siege of the Old City, he met a London girl, Esther Cailingold, who told him about her family just before she was shot and fatally wounded. Two years later, while in London on a Zionist mission, he went to pay his respects to her parents. There he met her younger sister, Mimi, and both fell in love. They travelled back to Kibbutz Lavi, married, and made a life together, returning in due course to London as Ambassador Avner and lady.

From the kibbutz, he left to become a journalist, then later joined the Foreign Office. He served in New York and at the Embassy in Washington; for ten years he worked in the Prime Minister's office as a close advisor to three Prime Ministers: Rabin, Begin and Peres. Begin, for whom Avner would often

Ambassador Yehuda Avner ready to present his credentials at the Palace, 1983 (Courtesy: Jewish Chronicle)

prepare English-language speeches, referred to him as 'my Shakespeare'.

Before leaving for London as Ambassador he did two things: he went to pray at the Kotel, and he paid a visit to Shlomo Argov at Hadassa. 'It is an impossible act to follow you, I make no pretence', he told Argov.

On his arrival, he met the leaders of the British community. Many of them had been personal friends with whom he had maintained warm links since the days of his *aliyah*. His arrival in London coincided with a stormy period in Anglo-Israeli relations, during the Israeli invasion of Lebanon. He had to put Israel's case not only to Whitehall but also to the

Ambassador and Mrs Avner at the reception following the accreditation

Sidney Harris

bewildered Jewish community. Night after night he was subjected to interrogation about the horrific pictures showing Israel as oppressor and in a harsh light. He appealed to the community 'to display a spirit of unity and solidarity with Israel in its current difficulties'.

Then followed the days of the Intifada. In a fighting article in *The Times* on 17 October 1988, he tried bravely to defend the Israeli Government.

> Imagine what a mere fraction of the Arab oil revenues could do to remove the squalor of Gaza and other refugee camps. Instead they are left to languish as an ongoing political and propaganda weapon against Israel. It is our view that the future of the peace process depends upon the restoration of law and order and the encouragement of the voice of moderation.

Like Argov before him, Avner was active in the Press in rebutting accusations against Israel, countering an onslaught

The Avners at home
receiving new olim, 1984
(Courtesy: Jewish
Chronicle)

that could be virulent at times. He travelled extensively around
the country pleading Israel's case to all Jewish communities and
the general public. He devoted much of his time to furthering
trade and investment links between the two countries.

During Avner's tenure, Prime Minister Shamir paid an
official visit to London. Mrs Shulamit Shamir was entertained
by Mrs Avner to tea at the Residence with the ladies of the
Embassy. Mrs Thatcher also paid her much acclaimed visit to

Ambassador Avner
meeting leaders of the
community in Ilford,
1984

Israel, the first British Prime Minister to do so. It was the culmination of a period of strong and friendly Anglo-Israeli relations, and in December 1987 President Herzog enjoyed a week's stay in Britain. Following the customary colourful welcome and the bouquet of flowers from Mrs Thatcher awaiting them at their hotel, President and Aura Herzog attended many meetings and functions. One of the most meaningful was a dinner at Lincoln's Inn where the President had once studied law and was made an Honorary Bencher on the occasion. He met the Lord Chancellor at the House of Lords; he met politicians and prominent intellectuals, from Harold Pinter to Sir Claus Moser; attended a glittering function at the Guildhall and met Dorothy de Rothschild to thank her for her munificent donations for the building of the Knesset and the new Supreme Court in Jerusalem. He addressed hundreds of Jewish youth urging them to make *aliyah*. Mrs Herzog enjoyed a lunch in her honour at the Residence.

Mrs Avner, originally a Londoner, was active in her own right in support of women's organisations, addressing them on many occasions and opening the Residence to their meetings.

Among the many happy functions at the Residence during this period were musical evenings, such as that on 20 February 1987 to mark the second anniversary of the British–Israel Arts Foundation, under the energetic chairmanship of Mrs Lilian Hochhauser, at which the Ambassador and Mrs Avner were the hosts and the baritone Raphael Frieder gave a recital. On 29 May 1987 there was another musical attended by Foreign Office guests, other ambassadors and leaders of the Jewish Community to honour Ewen Fergusson on his appointment as British Ambassador to France. Prior to this appointment, Ewen Fergusson had been in charge of the Middle East desk at the Foreign Office and had been very supportive and helpful at difficult times, such as during the Vanunu affair. I was also a guest at one of these musical evenings and was seated next to Jaqueline du Pré who was regularly invited to the Residence until the last weeks of her life.

On the evening of a recital in honour of the Israel Philharmonic Orchestra, Maestro Zubin Mehta was present.

At the end of the concert he got up and gave an improvised speech, all in Lithuanian Yiddish. Everyone was rolling on the floor with laughter. At a musical soirée in June 1986 in honour of Sir Antony Acland who had just been appointed the next British Ambassador to Washington, Ambassador Avner remarked that 'objectivity for Israelis is agreeing with everything we say', to which Sir Antony replied that 'understatement is an Israeli habit'. The music on that occasion was played by the British winner of the Israeli international harp contest, the young Welshman, Ieuan Jones.

The Avner's daughter, Yael, who was the only one of their four children to live in the Residence (for a year, in fact), married an Israeli from the Embassy. The wedding had been a family affair in Israel but was followed by a reception in London for the many family and friends among the Anglo-Jewish community – Yehuda Avner is the only Israeli Ambassador to Britain with brothers and sisters and an extended family still living in Manchester. At this reception, Chaim Topol was among the guests and entertained the party with charming stories and song. There was also a Shabbat lunch for Natan Sharansky following his release from Siberia, when after *birkat hamazon*, the Ambassador and the Guest of Honour embraced and danced at the head of the table.

The Avners are a religious and observant family. They brought to the Residence more of the spirit of Jewish life and traditional orthodoxy. I believe that they were the first to use the paved platform at the corner of the garden for a *sukkah*. On each evening of the Festival of Succot, guests would join them for the meal in the small crowded *sukkah* – friends, Embassy colleagues; weather-permitting, Yehuda would lead the singing and rejoicing. At Shevuot, they used to hold a study-night at the Residence with a minyan according to tradition in honour of the giving of the Torah.

They were also the first to establish a strictly kosher regime and trained the Portuguese housekeeper in all the intricacies of kashrut. They managed to send her on a cordon bleu course and she also learned to adapt her skills to Jewish dietary requirements. Ever since, the Portuguese lady has been punctilious in supervising the observation of kashrut among the successive ambassadors' wives.

70

The Avners building and decorating the sukkah

71

Ambassador Avner completed his tour of duty in Britain and Ireland in September 1988. Before leaving for Israel, he paid his respects at Buckingham Palace where he was determined to thank the Queen for 'the protection Britain has afforded me. Brave men and women have made it possible for me, a religious Jew, to walk to synagogue every week.' In rain or shine, one could meet the Ambassador progressing from the Residence, sometimes to a distant synagogue, with the guards at his heels. He summed up his five years of duty in London:

> It was an enormous privilege and a unique experience for me to be appointed Ambassador to the land of my birth. It has given me an intimate relationship with the Jewish community. I have come to feel I am a son of this community, of this country.

Ambassador Yoav Biran, 1988–1993

Yoav Biran, the former minister at the Embassy, Chargé d'Affaires when Ambassador Argov was shot in 1982, succeeded Yehuda Avner in 1988.

On the day before he left for London, Mr Biran went to take leave of Shlomo Argov, still paralysed at Hadassa Hospital. 'It was heartwarming to see that despite his condition, he gave me a genuine smile when I told him I was leaving for London. He said he was very happy for me and gave me his blessing for my success.'

He and Mr Argov were close friends. 1982 was a traumatic period; staff at the Embassy had been devastated. He had had to run the everyday work while the Lebanon war was raging, and this in addition to the personal pain he felt. Throughout the period he would visit Argov in hospital on a daily basis. He became one of the family; they would sit at Argov's bedside and talk to him as if he were conscious. The hours of one-sided, silent conversation left Biran drained, exhausted. He took over the ambassadorial duties and carried them impressively. He won the admiration of his colleagues and at the Ministry in Jerusalem. On his return home in November

1983, he was selected as the 'outstanding civil-servant of the year' and given the prize by President Yitzhak Navon.

Yoav Biran was born in Tel Aviv and holds an MA from the Hebrew University. In his diplomatic career, he served in a number of African countries. His experience in London was, nevertheless, extensive: from November 1977 to 1982, he served as Minister Plenipotentiary in London before becoming Chargé d'Affaires. When he returned to London as Ambassador on 2 November 1988 it was on Balfour Day, the anniversary of the Declaration and 'one of Britain's finest hours', as he noted at the time. A few months later, he presented his credentials as non-resident Ambassador to Ireland. One of the main subjects under discussion with the Irish leaders was the creation of a permanent Embassy, Ireland by then being the only country in western Europe where Israel did not enjoy full diplomatic recognition (on account of differences between the two countries, particularly as regards the role of UNIFIL and the Irish battalion in Lebanon). Like all Israeli ambassadors, he saw his position as having a dual role. 'I am an ambassador not just to Britain but also to the community and I look forward to a frank and open dialogue.'

Ambassador Yoav Biran ready to present his credentials at the Palace, 1988 (Courtesy: Jewish Chronicle)

Mr Biran arrived at the Residence alone, having divorced his wife Daniella. When in July 1991 he remarried, the Press reported: 'A diplomatic marriage is announced for Ambassador Biran and Mrs Moonman'. Jane Moonman, who used to be director of the British–Israel Public Affairs Committee, and the Ambassador had been friends for a number of years. Jane had worked vigorously for Soviet Jewry and was also chairman of Na'amat (the Labour women's organisation). She had been closely involved in work at the Embassy promoting Israel's case in Britain. They decided to get married in Jerusalem at Yemin Moshe and the British Ambassador, Mark Elliott, was among the guests.

The Residence was not unfamilar to Jane; she had been a guest on many occasions – such as an Independence Day gathering or when Masha Lubetsky, Chairman of International Na'amat was Mrs Argov's guest of honour. She had seen the house but never imagined the change in her life which would bring her to live in it. And now, as the Ambassador's new wife, she was 'literally carried over the doorstep'.

She made many improvements in the Residence, new furnishings and, more importantly, her 'bequest to future generations of Israeli ambassadors and their guests', a renovated cloakroom which had apparently not been touched since the house was first built and which had resembled a Victorian public toilet.

During their residence, the Birans entertained President and Mrs Herzog, the Rabins, Shimon Peres, David Levy, and many others. They served in London during momentous days of the successive waves of the Soviet *aliyah*. The gates were opened and Israel welcomed day after day thousands of Russia's Jews, young and old. As the joke went at the time, those who were not carrying a violin case were pianists! Many of the arriving musicians played to audiences in private homes and at schools. Some were taken in by Jewish communities abroad. Mrs Biran's favourite events at the Residence were the musical soirées featuring these new immigrant musicians from the Soviet Union.

Another event remembered fondly by the Birans was the dinner party held to celebrate Lord Weidenfeld's seventieth birthday. Prominent among the guests were the Chief Rabbi, Lord Jakobovits, Sir Patrick Wright, Permanent Under Secretary of State at the Foreign Office, Conrad Black and Minister Zvulun Hammer from Israel.

The Independence Day celebrations on the forty-fourth anniversary on 15 May 1992 caused traffic havoc throughout the neighbourhood. The star of the show was Mrs Thatcher who had never before appeared at Independence Day receptions. She came through the waiting crowds and uttered the words: 'I'm so sorry, I've forgotten my invitation'. On this occasion, the Security Guards were not so strict and recognised the guest and allowed her in. There she met the Russian Ambassador, the former Soviet Foreign Minister, Boris Pankin, Douglas Hogg, and the Representative of the Vatican, among some 900 other guests.

In its farewell editorial in the *Jewish Chronicle*, on his departure in October 1993, we read:

> Yoav Biran returns to Jerusalem after 5 years in London during which he has managed his dual ambassadorship – to Her majesty's Government and to the Jewish community – with intelligence, warmth and immense diplomatic skill. He has represented three different Israeli governments – Likud, National Unity and Labour – on issues ranging from the Intifada and the Gulf War to security and the Peace Process.'

Words that summarize and reflect so well the work of Ambassador Biran.

Ambassador Moshe Raviv and Mrs Hana Raviv, 1993–1997

'History teaches us that men and nations behave wisely once they have exhausted all other alternatives.' (Abba Eban, 1970)

We arrived in London a month after the famous handshake on the lawn of the White House, after the signing of the Oslo Agreements, in an atmosphere of hope and excitement. It was a momentous time of historic reconciliation between Israel and the Palestinians and we all felt part of those wonderful and challenging days. It was our third tour of duty in London. In the 1960s, as a young couple, we served at the Embassy during the time of Ambassador Lourie who was godfather at the birth of our son, Ilan, in London. Our daughter Orna was also born here. On our return to Israel, Moshe then became political secretary to Foreign Minister Eban. He served next as political councillor in Washington for six years. Subsequently, he became Ambassador to the Philippines (with responsibilities in Hong Kong as well). Our second tour of duty in London followed when Moshe was Minister Plenipotentiary (1983–1988). Returning to Israel, he was appointed Deputy Director-General for Information and in the following years became closely involved in the peace negotitations which started at the Madrid Conference in 1991.

Although we were returning to a familiar place, nothing compares with the responsibilities of an ambassador. Part of his role was to continue to build on the work of his predecessors and here he was following Ambassadors Avner and Biran. But priorities change according to the issues that emerge at the time and each ambassador brings his own style to bear when giving priority to those that predominate. Thus Ambassador Raviv emphasised in his work the importance of consolidating support for the peace process both among the general public and within the Jewish community. Much of his time in the first months was devoted to this subject, trying to to reach members of Parliament of all parties as well as the wider public. Recognising the importance of the media in

Sidney Harris

modern diplomacy, he devoted considerable time to radio and television, explaining Israeli policy and promoting trade, investment and tourism to Israel.

The dialogue between the two governments was very fruitful and was consolidated through mutual visits. Prime Minister John Major and his wife visited Israel and so did Foreign Minister Malcolm Rifkind and Defence Minister

Ambassador Moshe Raviv ready to present his credentials at the Palace, 1993

Michael Portillo and others. Prime Minister Yitzhak Rabin visited Britain as did Shimon Peres. Following the change of government in 1996, Prime Minister Binyamin Netanyahu and his wife Sarah made their first visit to Britain. During our tenure both Leaders of the Opposition, John Smith (as I have described) and Tony Blair, visited Israel. These official visits were reflected in the life of the Residence where meetings, lunches, teas were held at which wives of the visiting guests were entertained and introduced to members of women's organisations and the community.

Although the Residence is a separate building and at a different address, it is but an extension of the Embassy. All that happens there and takes place in the field of diplomacy is felt immediately at the Residence. When the Embassy was damaged by a car bomb, not only were more policemen

Ambassador and Mrs Raviv returning from the Palace

Sidney Harris

78

posted outside the Residence, we all went through the shock and distress of the blast.

There have been many moments of elation in recent life at the Residence: when we watched the signing of the peace treaty with Jordan in the Arava, when we hosted a dinner at which for the first time the Ambassadors from Jordan and Morocco were present.

There were also days of sadness, anguish and grief, when we were glued to the television to watch the funeral of our Prime Minister, for us a painful personal loss as well. The assassination of Yitzhak Rabin was certainly the most traumatic experience of our time at 58 Avenue Road.

Prime Minister Yitzhak Rabin and Mrs Leah Rabin with the Ravivs, 1994

79

Her Majesty the Queen with President Weizman and Ambassador Raviv at a Reception at Spencer House on the occasion of the State Visit of President and Mrs Weizman

The State Visit

One of the highlights has been the official visit of President Ezer Weizman and his wife. During our time they came twice to Britain. The first of these occasions was when the President, a former RAF pilot and participant in the battles that took place, came to represent Israel at the fiftieth anniversary of the end of the Second World War in Europe, in May 1995. The second was when he enjoyed the full honour of the first State Visit of an Israeli President to the UK. As guests of Her Majesty the Queen, the President and his wife stayed at Buckingham Palace. To see the Israeli flag alongside the Union Jack in Whitehall and along the Mall was a very emotional experience!

The Ravivs preparing to go to the Diplomatic Ball at the Palace

The Ravivs with Emeritus Chief Rabbi Lord Jakobovits and Lady Jakobovits

Sidney Harris

81

Sidney Harris

Neighbours

For as long as the Israeli flag has been flying on this house, that of Pakistan has been flying next door at No. 56 and, while formal diplomatic relations have never existed between our countries, good neighbourly relations have always prevailed.

For the fifty years since the creation of Pakistan in 1947, the High Commissioner has resided in Avenue Road. The proximity is great; between the two houses the aroma of curry mingles with the aroma of chicken soup. The English proverb says: 'good fences make good neighbours'. The fences between the two homes are of thick green trees and shrubs which nonetheless allow for the exchange of goodwill between the residents.

The stories of this relationship go back to the time of the first Ambassador, Mr Elath. At that time the High Commissioner was Mr Mohamed Ikramullah. He had six young children and they were like family for the young Prince Hassan, brother of King Hussein, at that time Crown Prince of Jordan.

82

He was at boarding school in England and he used to spend his holidays with the children at 56 Avenue Road, the two families being close friends. In spite of the fence, the balls from the garden used to fly on to the Israeli Residence lawn, and young Prince Hassan used to run round to fetch them. Many times he was reprimanded by the Pakistani staff and told not to go into 'Israeli territory'. One day the ball rolled into the middle of the street outside. Little Bitlan, the then six-year old daughter of the High Commissioner, ran after it without noticing a cab driving at speed towards her. By good fortune, Ambassador Elath, going out at the gate for a walk (in those days of the late 1950s, an Israeli ambassador could still venture forth without four guards and two cars to accompany him) jumped straight to the middle of the road and picked the frightened girl up when the cab came to a sudden halt next to them. Years later this small girl became the wife of Prince Hassan, now Crown Prince of Jordan. She is now Princess Sarwath and told me this story herself at a dinner in London following the establishment of diplomatic relations between Jordan and Israel. For many years the story was told and retold in her family how the Israeli Ambassador had saved the life of little Bitlan. Her father passed away, but her mother, a well-known writer in Pakistan, became Ambassador to Morocco and was active in the political life of her country.

In 1994, when the Embassy at Palace Green was bombed, a huge bouquet of white flowers was delivered to the Residence; attached was a heartening note of good wishes from our Pakistani neighbours. When there was a change of High Commissioner, we as good neighbours baked a cake and sent it with a letter of welcome and good wishes. The next day, a box of sweet mangoes from Pakistan arrived with a fine letter of appreciation and thanks. I hope that these disclosures do not cause embarrassment, and that the fact that their Excellencies took tea together and conversed as neighbours will not provoke a diplomatic incident.

We also recall a few occasions when both residences held functions on the same evening. Some of our guests entered the next driveway and found themselves at the wrong party; they made their apologies and left to come to us and had to make further apologies for their late arrival which had had us worried.

We hope that the day is not far distant when the two Ambassadors and their wives will be able to visit and enjoy each other's company, and not have to send letters and gifts through go-betweens; then the good fence will make really good neighbours.

The legacy of the house

As we celebrate the jubilee of the establishment of Israel, the blue and white flag will fly for the fiftieth time over 58 Avenue Road.

What an incredible journey in only a hundred years. From the dreams of the 'pilgrimage' of Herbert Bentwich to the realisation of that dream! As Herzl wrote in his diary of 1897: 'At Basle I founded the Jewish State. If I said this loudly today, I would be greeted by universal laughter. Perhaps in five years, certainly in fifty years, everyone will perceive it.' Fifty years and 85 days later, the United Nations approved the partitition of Palestine, thereby clearing the way for the creation of Israel.

The house at 58 Avenue Road has echoed these events, from the days of the launching of political Zionism to the days of its triumph and realisation. Destiny it seems brought me on this fiftieth anniversary to this famous site.

In this house, one feels the breath of history. If it is time for me to halt this journey through the stories of the house – from the Bentwich family 100 years ago, tales intertwined with Zionism and the Israeli experience – I know that the story will go on with new residents, new sounds, new colours. A house is not only the bricks that make it. It is a mosaic of the lives of all who live in it, who work, laugh and love in it, and make it, each in his own way 'a home away from home'.

Chronology of events

The Bentwich Family

1856 Herbert Bentwich born
1892 Bentwich family moved to 58 Avenue Road
1895 Thelma Yellin born
1896 Publication of Herzl's *Der Judenstaat*
1897 Herbert Bentwich and Maccabaean Pilgrimage to
        Palestine
        First Zionist Congress in Basle
1913 First Bentwich children settled at Zichron Ya'akov
        Bentwich family moved from Avenue Road to
        Cavendish Road
1915 Susanna Bentwich died
1917 Balfour Declaration
1920 Thelma Yellin settled in Jerusalem
1922 British Mandate in Palestine
1925 Establishment of Hebrew University in Jerusalem
1929 Herbert Bentwich settled in Eretz Israel
1932 Herbert Bentwich died in Jerusalem
1997 Exhibition of Muriel Bentwich's pictures at Mane-
        Katz Museum, Haifa

From Mandate to Independence

1947
November 29   Adoption by UN General Assembly of Resolu-
              tion for Partition of Palestine

1948
May 14   Declaration of Israeli Independence
May 15   Arab invasion

Wars, Diplomacy and Peace Initiatives

1951

September   UN Security Council Resolution on Freedom of Passage in Suez Canal

1956

October 29   Sinai Campaign, attempt to secure free passage for Israel in Suez Canal and Gulf of Aqaba

1958

July   Assassination of King Feisal of Iraq
Foreign Minister Golda Meir met Secretary of State in London

August   Turning-point in relations between Britain and Israel when Israel allowed passage over its airspace to British planes bearing troops and equipment in support of King Hussein when threatened by Egypt
First meeting between Prime Minister Harold Macmillan and Prime Minister David Ben-Gurion in London

1960

March 4   Shimon Peres, Deputy Minister of Defence, met John Profumo, Minister of State at Foreign Office: Britain agreed to sell Israel 60 Centurion tanks and two submarines

1967

May 25   Prime Minister Harold Wilson assured Israeli Foreign Minister, Abba Eban, of Britain's support for free passage through Straits of Tiran

June 5–10   Six Day War

November 22   UN Resolution 242 formulated by Lord Caradon, British Ambassador to UN, adopted unanimously: establishing positions and principles for an agreement between Israel and the Arab States
George Brown, British Foreign Minister,

	clarified terms of the resolution: 'Israel will withdraw from territories', not the Territories
1970	Death of President Nasser of Egypt, succeeded by Anwar Sadat

1973

October 6	Yom Kippur War Israel eventually recovered Golan Heights and part of West Bank of Suez Canal
October 22	UN Security Council Resolution 338 called for cease-fire and disengagement; Geneva Conference involving all parties in the war

1974

May of forces	Israel, Egypt and Syria accept disengagement
June	Resignation of government of Golda Meir, Yitzhak Rabin formed his first government

1977

November 17	Prime Minister Menahem Begin announced visit of President Sadat to the Knesset
November 20	President Sadat addressed the Knesset
December 2–4	Prime Minister Begin paid Official Visit to Britain
December 20	Begin met Prime Minister Callaghan and representative of French President Guiscard d'Esting in London to discuss Israel's peace plans

1978

May	Foreign Minister Moshe Dayan visited Britain and Scandinavia
July 17	Leeds Castle Conference between Moshe Dayan, Kamel Hassan (Egypt) and US Secretary of State Cyrus Vance to discuss plan for five-year transition on question of sovereignty for Gaza and West Bank
September 17	Camp David Agreement between Israel and Egypt signed at the White House
December 8	Death of Golda Meir

December 10	Award of Nobel Peace Prize to Prime Minister Begin and President Sadat

1979

February	British Foreign Secretary Dr David Owen visited Israel for talks
March 26	The Israel–Egypt Peace Treaty signed at the White House
May	Prime Minister Begin met Prime Minister Margaret Thatcher in London with Cyrus Vance

1980

May	Foreign Minister Yitzhak Shamir visited London for talks

1981

October 6	Assassination of President Sadat
October 16	Moshe Dayan died

1982

March 29	Visit of Foreign Secretary Lord Carrington to Israel
June 3	Israel Ambassador Shlomo Argov attacked in London
June 6	Israeli army invaded Lebanon to attack PLO bases under operation 'Peace for Galilee'
June 7	Clashes with the Syrian army
July 4	Siege of Beirut and withdrawal of PLO

1983

May 17	Ceasefire agreement between Israel and Lebanon signed in Khalde and Kiryat Shmona

1984

March	President Chaim Herzog paid private visit to Britain as guest of Jewish community (unveiled centenary plaque at Sir Moses Montefiore's home, 99 Park Lane); received by the Queen and had talks with Prime Minister
September	Shimon Peres formed government of national unity

1985

February   Israel Defence Forces left Lebanon

1986

January   Prime Minister Peres made visits to Britain
             and the Netherlands

May   Prime Minister Thatcher made official visit to
             Israel

1987

December   Start of Palestinian Intifada

1989

May   Prime Minister Shamir made official visit to
             Britain for talks with Prime Minister and
             Foreign Secretary, Geoffrey Howe

November   Dismantling of the Berlin Wall

1990

October   Foreign Secretary Douglas Hurd visited Israel
             for talks with Foreign Minister David Levy

1991

January   Gulf War, Israel hit by Iraqi scud missiles

August   Collapse of Soviet Union

October   Prime Minister Shamir attended Middle East
             Peace Conference in Madrid

1992

January   Foreign Minister David Levy attended
             Multilateral Middle East Peace Talks in
             Moscow

July   Yitzhak Rabin formed government

December   Prime Minister Rabin visited Britain for talks
             with Prime Minister John Major and senior
             ministers

1993

September 13 Israel–PLO Declaration of Principles signed at
             the White House

1994

January   Foreign Minister Hurd visited Israel

May 19	Prime Minister Rabin and King Hussein held secret talks in London
May 26	Britain lifted 12-year embargo on arms sales to Israel
July 25–26	Prime Minister Rabin and King Hussein signed Declaration ending state of war between Israel and Jordan in ceremony at the White House
July 26	Car bomb explosions at Embassy of Israel and JIA offices in London
October 18	Prime Minister Rabin visited London for talks with Prime Minister Major, broken off following Hamas suicide attack in Tel Aviv
October 20	Visit to Israel by Defence Secretary Malcolm Rifkind
October 26	Israel–Jordan Peace Treaty signed in the Arava at ceremony attended by President Clinton
October 30	Economic Summit for Middle East and North Africa opened in Casablanca by King Hassan II in presence of Prime Minister Rabin, Foreign Minister Peres and other world leaders
December 10	Nobel Peace Prize awarded to Prime Minister Rabin, Foreign Minister Peres and Chairman Arafat

1995

November 4	Assassination of Prime Minister Rabin
November 6	Rabin's burial attended by leaders from 80 nations including Prime Minister Major, Prince Charles and opposition leader Tony Blair

1996

April 11	Operation 'Grapes of Wrath' launched against Hizbollah in Southern Lebanon
May 29	Elections for Prime Minister and the Knesset, Binyamin Netanyahu formed new government

1997

February	State Visit to Britain of President Ezer Weizman and Mrs Weizman

| *November* | Official Visit of Prime Minister Netanyahu for talks with Prime Minister Blair, Foreign Secretary Robin Cook and US Secretary of State Madeleine Albright |

Israeli Envoys in London

1948–49	Ivor Linton, unofficial representative of Israel
1949	Mordecai Eliash, Minister Plenipotentiary
1949–59	Eliahu Elath, First Ambassador
1960–65	Arthur Lourie
1965–70	Aharon Remez
1970–73	Michael Comay
1974–77	Gideon Rafael
1977–79	Avraham Kidron
1979–82	Shlomo Argov
1982–83	Yoav Biran, Chargé d'Affaires
1983–88	Yehuda Avner
1988–93	Yoav Biran
1993–97	Moshe Raviv

Bibliography

Archives of the *Jewish Chronicle*

Bartov, Hanoch: *An Israeli at the Court of St James's.* London: Vallentine Mitchell, 1971

Bermant, Chaim: *The Cousinhood.* London: Eyre & Spottiswoode, 1971

Bentwich, Margery: *Thelma Yellin, pioneer musician.* Jerusalem: R. Mass, 1964

Bentwich, Norman de Mattos, and Bentwich, Margery: *Herbert Bentwich, the pilgrim father.* Jerusalem: Hozaath Ivrith Ltd., 1940

Bentwich, Norman de Mattos: *My 77 years – 1883–1960: an account of my life and times.* London: Routledge & Kegan Paul, 1962

Bentwich, Norman de Mattos: *Wanderer between two worlds.* London: Kegan Paul, Trench, Trubner, 1941

Bentwich, Norman de Mattos: 'The Wanderers and other Jewish scholars of my youth', *Trans. J.H.S.E.,* XX, 1964, 51–62

Cesarani, David: *The Jewish Chronicle and Anglo-Jewry, 1841–1991.* Cambridge: Cambridge University Press, 1994

Eban, Abba: *Personal witness: Israel through my eyes.* London: Cape, 1993

Elath, Eliahu: *Mi-ba'ad la-'arafel ha-yamim: pirké zikhronot (Through the mist of the times: reminiscences)* [In Hebrew]. Jerusalem: Yad Izhak Ben Zvi, 1989

Eyre, Alan Montague: *St John's Wood, its houses, its haunts and its celebrities.* London: Chapman & Hall, 1913

Margetson, Stella: *St John's Wood: an abode of love and the arts.* London: Home and Law Publishing, 1988

Sieff, Marcus: *Don't ask the price: the memoirs of the president of Marks & Spencer.* London: Weidenfeld & Nicolson, 1986